The (Almost)
No Fat
Holiday

Cookbook

Festive Vegetarian Recipes

Bryanna Clark Grogan

Book Publishing Company Summertown, Tennessee

Cover Photo by John Harper
Interior design by Sheryl Karas
Illustrations by Warren Jefferson

Printed in the United States by Book Publishing Company
P.O. Box 99
Summertown, TN 38483

99 98 97   4 3 2

ISBN 1-57067 009-9

Grogan, Bryanna Clark, 1948
         The almost no fat holiday cookbook: festive vegetarian recipes /
    by Bryanna Clark Grogan
         p. cm.
         Includes bibliographical references and index.
         ISBN 1-57067-009-9 (alk. paper)
         1. Vegetarian cookery. 2. Low-fat cookery-Recipes. 3. Holiday
    cookery. 4. Menus. l. Tide.
    TX837.G6763 1995
    641.5'636-dc20   95-10914
                                                          CIP

To my wonderful family
who makes holidays a joy.

Acknowledgements
Many thanks to Drs. Dean Ornish, Neal Barnard, Julian Whitaker, and John McDougall for leading the way. Also, thanks to John Robbins and Dr. Michael Klaper of EarthSave, the *Laurel's Kitchen* gang, and The Farm people for inspiring millions to the vegetarian way of life, and to Frances Moore Lappé for her pioneering work.

Table of Contents

About the Author

Bryanna Clark Grogan has been a food writer and teacher for over 20 years. Her interest in cooking began before she can even remember, and having her first child sparked a lifelong interest in nutrition. She has four children, two stepsons, two foster sons, numerous grandchildren, and a large extended family (a "small" family get-together might number 18-20!).

Bryanna contributes frequently to *Vegetarian Times* magazine, is working on several books, and is a part-time librarian. She lives with husband Brian (her faithful recipe tester) and several children on idyllic Denman Island, off the east coast of Vancouver Island in British Columbia.

Introduction

One of my favorite pastimes is developing menus for family holiday meals. My children have certain expectations, and my new family members have others. My own priorities changed when I became a vegetarian and again when I adopted the no-fat-added style of cooking recommended by Drs. Dean Ornish, Neal Barnard, and John McDougall for heart health, lifetime weight control, and prevention of many degenerative diseases. Add to this the personal likes and dislikes of a large extended family, and I'm presented with quite a challenge!

If you find yourself in a similar situation and are tempted to send out for pizza (no cheese, of course!), this book is for you. No doubt you'll serve a few traditional, higher-fat favorites that just can't be revised to your satisfaction, but my goal is to create an almost-no-fat meal that can stand on its own and that doesn't taste and feel like "spa food." (There's nothing wrong with "spa food," but we want our holiday food to feel festive and substantial!) Your guests who are on very restricted diets can then eat to their heart's content, and everyone else can indulge in the extras knowing that most of the meal is almost fat-free.

And, by the way, there's no need to save these recipes only for holidays—I hope that you will incorporate some of them into your daily meals, using some of my suggestions or your own imagination for variations that may or may not be traditional.

In addition to the traditional, North American secular, Christian, and Jewish holidays, such as Christmas, Passover, and Independence Day, I've included menus and recipes for some of the Muslim, Buddhist, Baha'i, and Hindu feast days. Because our North American cultural mosaic has become ever more complex, I like to celebrate the holidays of other lands and religions, not only out of respect, but also to increase my family's awareness of these cultural riches.

By studying about and participating in some of the festivals that seem strange to us, but are dear to our immigrant neighbors, we learn not only about the contrasts between us, but also about the similarities. There's the universal love of feasting, wearing special clothes, and making merry, or the patterns that run through certain seasonal holidays worldwide (candles and greenery for mid-winter festivals; pranks, bonfires, and night-time parties at autumnal holidays; dressing up and making lots of noise to bring in the New Year; or the use of eggs as a spring symbol).

It is my hope that, as citizens of the world, we can rejoice equally in the differences that make us unique and in the common values, sentiments, and festive themes that tie us together, for we are really very much more similar than we are different.

To avoid imposing Christian concepts on other faiths, we use the abbreviations C.E.

◇◇

(Common Era) instead of A.D. (Anno Domini or Year of the Lord) and B.C.E. (before the Common Era) instead of B.C. (before Christ).

The Occasional Use Of High-Fat Ingredients

Nowhere in this book will you find the use of meat, fish, poultry, eggs, or dairy products. Oil is used only to grease pans and in one recipe for a low-fat pastry. I have included several no-fat "pastries," but for some traditional recipes, this oil pastry, containing half the fat of ordinary pastry, is preferable for special occasions. You can often cut the fat in the recipe further by using only one crust. Of course, the use of this pastry is entirely optional.

I have tried to avoid the use of high-fat seeds and nuts wherever possible, but there may be some added to very traditional recipes where no substitute will do, or where their omission would completely change the character of the dish. These recipes are also for optional use.

How Much Fat is Too Much?

You're apt to see the quantity of fat in a food measured as a *percentage of calories* in that food. This is because nutritionists are recommending what proportion of calories in our diet should come from fat. Standard recommendations for good health are currently 30% of calories from fat; recent reports from researchers recommend much lower levels—around 10% to 15%—to achieve weight loss and protect against heart disease and cancer.

After eating a low-fat diet for a while, you probably won't need to count fat grams at all, but in the beginning, it might help you to see how much fat you are eating (or how little). A moderately active man weighing about 150 lbs. can eat about 25 grams of fat a day to stay in the 10%-calories-from-fat range; a moderately active woman weighing 130 lbs. can eat 20 grams daily. If you are less active, eat a couple of grams less; if you are more active, you can eat a few more. If your ideal weight is more or less than this, adjust your fat intake accordingly.

It's not too difficult to calculate the percentage of calories from fat that you eat each day. A gram of fat will provide 9 calories when consumed. If over a day's time you've eaten 20 grams of fat and 1800 calories, you can calculate the percentage of calories from fat like this:

> 20 grams fat X 9 calories per gram = 180 calories from fat
>
> 180 calories from fat/1800 total calories = 10% of calories from fat

This is a fairly easy example to calculate. When the numbers get more complicated, (72 grams of fat and 2330 calories, for example), round up a little and get a close approximation (multiply fat grams by 10 instead of 9, so that 72 grams x 10 = 720 calories; 720 calories is a little less than 1/3 of 2330, so the percentage is around 30%).

Although considering the percentage of fat in your total diet can be useful, looking at individual foods or recipes this way can be misleading. A food can be low in fat, but be so low in calories as well that the *percentage* of fat to calories can look deceivingly high (as with regular tofu, which has only 82 calories in a 4 oz. serving, but half those calories come from fat). A calorie-dense food, such as one high in sugar, might have a lower *percentage* of calories from fat, but actually contain more fat per serving. If you planned on eating quite a bit of just one food, you might want to look at the percentage of calories from fat in that one food, but we rarely eat like this. The best way to keep your fat level down to about 10% of total calories is to follow the nutrition guide on pages 8-9, don't use added oils and fats, eat only plant foods, and keep high-fat plant foods to a bare minimum.

Tofu deserves some additional mention because so much has been written about its high percentage of fat. As I demonstrated in the previous paragraph, 50% of the calories in regular tofu come from fat. But the total amount of calories in tofu are very low, much lower than equivalent amounts of avocado, nuts, etc., and much lower than eggs, oil, and solid cooking fats. When I use 1 lb. of regular tofu in my basic cake recipe for 18 cupcakes, each cupcake has about 1 gram of fat (and reduced-fat tofu lowers it even more). A traditional, "low-fat" recipe for 12 cupcakes or muffins made with 1 large egg and ¼ cup of oil (not counting any nuts that might be added) would contain about 58 grams of fat or close to 5 grams per cupcake or muffin.

The truth is that soy foods are good for us. Study after study confirms that soy foods of all kinds can significantly lower blood cholesterol, are an excellent source of iron in the diet, and may have a major role in cancer prevention.

Tofu is probably the most versatile soy food since it can be used not only as meat substitute, but also as a replacement for high-fat dairy products and eggs. Also, tofu and soymilk provide a natural way to ingest unprocessed, essential fatty acids without the need for expensive oil supplements. As long as fruits, vegetables, whole grains, and legumes make up the majority of your diet (and nuts, oils, seeds, olives, and avocados are only occasional treats), tofu, soymilk, and other soy foods can play important supporting roles.

If you are still concerned about the fat in tofu and soy foods, investigate the lower-fat soy products that are coming into the market: reduced-fat soymilk, tofu, and silken tofu. I have used reduced-fat tofu throughout the book to demonstrate how you can use it to cut back on fat even more than with regular tofu.

If you cannot find reduced-fat soy products in your area, you may substitute the full-fat products without affecting the outcome of the recipes, but the fat content will increase slightly.

There are many low-fat, vegetarian hot dogs and burgers on the market too, and textured vegetable protein is naturally almost fat-free (see page 169).

Dietary Fat for Children and Teenagers

Please note that although for many adults a very low-fat, fairly low-protein, high-fiber, vegetarian diet may be the best choice, children and teenagers need a higher-fat, higher-protein, and lower-fiber diet. They can eat the same foods that you do, but let them eat often, and add higher-fat foods (nut and seed butters, avocados) and high-protein foods (nuts, seeds, tofu, soymilk, and other soy products, beans, nutritional yeast, wheat germ) to make their diets *at least* 20% of calories from fat. Avoid excessive consumption of juice, soft drinks, and coffee.

Check the bibliography on page 185 for books that will give you more complete information on vegetarian nutrition for children.

A Word About Nutrition

A full discussion of nutrition is beyond the scope of this book. I urge you to consult the books listed in the bibliography so that you will have solid nutritional information to work with.

Here are a few things to keep in mind:

✔ Anyone who eats enough calories to maintain their body weight and energy level is getting enough protein (perhaps more than enough).

✔ As long as you eat a varied diet, you don't need to worry about combining proteins (eating beans and grains at the same meal, etc.)

✔ All known nutrients (with the possible exceptions of vitamin B_{12} and vitamin D) are adequately supplied by a *varied* diet of any whole, vegetarian foods which supply you with enough calories for good health. You can meet your requirement for vitamin B_{12} by taking 25 micrograms each week in pill form, or eating nutritional yeast flakes that have B_{12} added. If you expose your face and arms to the sun (even on a cloudy day) for 10 to 15 minutes a day, your body will naturally produce enough vitamin D. I recommend that you take some vitamin D from a vegetable source during the winter if you live in a northern climate or are nursing or pregnant.

✔ Over-consumption of protein, *not* under-consumption of calcium, may be an important factor contributing to osteoporosis. World health statistics show that the disease is most common in countries where dairy products are consumed in large quantities. Rich vegetarian sources of calcium are kale, dried legumes, sesame meal, blackstrap molasses, green leafy vegetables, carob, soy flour, tofu made with calcium salts (most commercial tofu is these days), dried fruit, nutritional yeast, corn tortillas and masa harina, acorn squash, and sea vegetables. If you are still concerned about calcium, take calcium carbonate, the cheapest, most concentrated, and easily absorbed form. Get plenty of exercise, avoid alcohol and tobacco, and reduce your consumption of caffeine and soft drinks.

✔ You do not need to eat red meat for iron. Some excellent vegetarian sources of iron are sea vegetables, prunes and other dried fruits, prune juice, nutritional yeast, blackstrap molasses, beans, soy foods, whole grains, potatoes, sesame meal, and fresh peas. Dairy products lack iron and can block iron absorption. Your iron absorption is increased by eating plenty of foods rich in vitamin C, such as fruits and vegetables, not drinking caffeinated beverages (including tea) with meals, and cooking in cast iron pots. The Chinese have excellent iron levels despite high levels of fiber and low levels of red meat in their diet.

If you are pregnant, nursing, ill, or under stress, you will need to include more concentrated proteins (tofu, tempeh, textured vegetable protein, other soy foods, and seitan). If you are expending large amounts of energy, you will need more grains, fruits, and high-carbohydrate vegetables.

Eat a variety of whole foods in as close to their natural state as possible.

Allergies, Soyfoods, and Alternatives

Most of the recipes in this book call for "reduced-fat" soymilk and tofu of various kinds. If you cannot find the "reduced-fat" variety in your area, you can use the ordinary varieties without affecting the outcome. The fat content per serving will be slightly higher.

To make homemade, "reduced-fat" soymilk, dilute 1 quart (4 cups) of regular, commercial, or homemade soymilk with 1½ cups water. (To fortify with calcium, add 1 tablespoon calcium carbonate powder to the resulting 5½ cups diluted soymilk, which will provide about 325 mg of calcium per cup. Shake the milk well before pouring.)

If you are allergic to soy products, you may substitute rice, almond, or potato-based, commercial, non-dairy milks for the soymilk—all are fairly low in fat. Tofu is more difficult to replace, but to a certain extent blended, cooked rice, millet, barley, oatmeal, and cornmeal can be used to replace it in creamy, blended mixtures such as shakes, puddings, and sauces, etc. Some experimentation is required.

Seitan, a wheat gluten product, or sometimes cooked beans can replace frozen tofu or textured vegetable (soy) protein.

See the glossary section on pages 182-84 for more information on foods you may be unfamiliar with.

Controversial Ingredients

For today's busy cooks, the use of commercial convenience foods is essential, but be cautious. Use breads, cereals, and crackers without added fats. Avoid products that are nothing more than fat-free junk food—full of sugar, salt, artificial flavors, sweeteners, fat substitutes, refined ingredients, and the like. Make use of quality commercial products like baked tortilla chips, fruit sorbets, and reduced-fat, non-dairy beverages and desserts, etc.

Salt can be reduced to your taste or replaced with salt substitutes or, in some cases, herbal blends. But be aware that commercially processed foods and cheese account for over 75% of salt in the American diet, so you may not need to reduce salt when eating unprocessed, dairy-free foods. You may wish to use a low-sodium (sometimes called "lite") soy sauce.

The use of *sugar* is always controversial. My take on it is that we get too complaisant when we eat "natural" sugars, such as concentrated grain or fruit sugars. Researchers have found that ingesting sugar in the form of sucrose, glucose, fructose, honey, or orange juice *all* led to a significant drop in the white blood cell index of the body, reducing the effectiveness of the immune system.

So, I leave it up to you. I eat desserts once a week at most, and I use Sucanat (granulated sugar cane juice) and turbinado sugar, an unbleached sugar. Use ordinary white and brown sugar if you like (cane sugars are bleached with bone ash, but beet sugar is not), or you can use granulated Fruitsource, a concentrated grain and fruit sweetener, if you prefer (this isn't as sweet as sugar). Honey and molasses (a good source of calcium and iron) lend special flavor to some desserts. You can substitute liquid Fruitsource, maple syrup, concentrated fruit syrup, or grain syrups for honey and molasses, but they are generally half as sweet as honey and far more costly.

Frozen fruit juice concentrates are an inexpensive sweetener for fruit desserts and some baking, replacing some of the liquid as well. The recipe must have a fair amount of liquid to start with. For each ½ cup sugar and 1½ cups liquid, substitute 1½ cups of frozen apple juice (a 12 oz. can) or other sweet, juice concentrate, adding 1 tsp. of baking soda to counteract the acid in the juice. To use less liquid, boil it down by half.

Alcoholic beverages, such as wine, beer, and liqueurs can add rich flavor to no-fat cooking. Most of the alcohol evaporates during cooking, but if you prefer, you can use a good-quality, non-alcoholic wine or beer, or in some cases, juice. Dry sherry can be replaced by a mixture of frozen apple juice concentrate and non-alcoholic dry white wine, or a fairly sweet, non-alcoholic wine. Apple, cranberry, or unsweetened white grape juice, or just plain water with a tablespoon or two of balsamic vinegar are other options. Liqueurs and hard liquor, such as brandy, rum, and whiskey, can often be replaced by an appropriate flavor extract, but use less extract than you would liqueur.

Coffee contains caffeine, a highly-addictive substance that can affect insulin balance, so I recommend the use of Swiss water-decaffeinated, organic coffee or a good coffee substitute. (I also use good-quality, water-decaffeinated tea.)

Artificial sweeteners or fats are not recommended and not used in this book. They simply keep your taste buds clamoring for more sweet, greasy foods, and the jury is not in yet on whether or not these products may be harmful.

Steam-Frying

One term that you will see over and over in my recipes is "steam-fry." It simply means sautéing or stir-frying without fat. To do this, use a heavy skillet, nonstick or lightly oiled with about ½ tsp. of oil brushed on with your fingertips, or a well-seasoned wok, oiled in the same way.

Heat your pan over high heat, add your chopped onions or other vegetables and one or two tablespoons of liquid (water, broth, or wine), depending on the amount of vegetables. Cook over high heat until the liquid starts to evaporate, stirring with a spatula or wooden spoon. Keep doing this until the vegetables are done to your liking; add *just enough* liquid to keep the vegetables from sticking to the bottom of the pan—you don't want to stew them!

You can brown onions perfectly by this method. As soon as the natural sugar in the onions starts to brown on the bottom and edges of the pan, add a little liquid and scrape the browned onions, mixing them into the liquids and around into the other cooking onions. Keep doing this until the onions are soft and brown, being careful not to scorch them.

Kitchen Equipment

You will need a blender for many recipes, but it doesn't need to be a fancy, expensive one. I would also recommend a food processor (again, it doesn't have to be an expensive one unless you plan to use it for bread dough). It will save you a great deal of time and effort with chopping, and it works much better than a blender for thick mixtures.

If you can, acquire a set of the new, nonstick pans, the ones with coatings that do not scrape off. Include some baking pans as well as sauté and saucepans—you can buy one at a time as you replace old pans. With these, you can bake and brown foods with no oil whatsoever.

❖❖

The (Almost)
No Fat
Holiday
Cookbook

Festive Vegetarian Recipes

◆◆◆

A Tex-Mex Brunch

There are several universal customs that link New Year's festivities from country to country—loud noisemaking; partying, feasting, and drinking; dressing up in costume or new clothes; paying off old debts; and eating beans! Yes, strange as it may seem, there is a long association between beans and good luck on New Year's Day.

In Japan, it is the custom for the head of the house to go through all of the rooms at midnight of New Year's Eve, scattering roasted beans about and chanting "Oni wa soto, fuka wa uchi" ("Out with the demons! In with the Luck!").

In Northern Europe, families or communities selected a King, and sometimes also a Queen, of Bean, "the nobilities of Misrule," who presided over games and revels.

In the Southern United States even today, it is customary to eat black-eyed peas, usually in the form of a dish called Hoppin' John, for good luck in the New Year. The spicy black-eyed peas and rice (with the greens that often accompany them) were brought to the South by African slaves. The English-Irish-Scottish slave-owners brought their Celtic and Anglo-Saxon customs of eating beans for good luck and hopping over the dying embers of New Year's bonfires, also for good luck. It seems reasonable to assume that this is the origin of the name Hoppin' John (the Anglo-Saxon word "hoppan" meant a religious dance or leap—a blending of African foods and European lore).

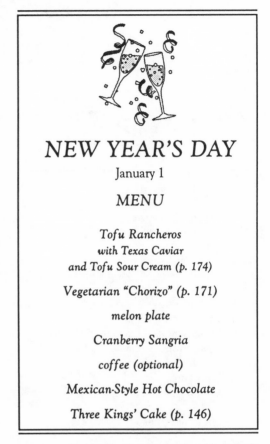

NEW YEAR'S DAY
January 1

MENU

Tofu Rancheros
with Texas Caviar
and Tofu Sour Cream (p. 174)

Vegetarian "Chorizo" (p. 171)

melon plate

Cranberry Sangria

coffee (optional)

Mexican-Style Hot Chocolate

Three Kings' Cake (p. 146)

I always liked the idea of a New Year's Day brunch to celebrate and bring in the new year in a casual and relaxed fashion—rather than serving another elaborate holiday dinner. This Tex-Mex brunch will wake up the most jaded appetites and introduce black-eyed peas to your guests in the form of a spicy salad or relish known as "Texas Caviar."

This menu could also be used for a Southwestern-style Christmas, Father's Day, or small wedding brunch.

Tofu Rancheros

*S*erve these spicy, Mexican-style tofu "omelets" with Texas Caviar, p. 17, Vegetarian "Chorizo," p. 171, and Tofu Sour Cream, p. 174, for a colorful and delicious main course.

"Omelets"
2 (10.5 oz.) pkgs. reduced-fat, extra-firm,
    SILKEN tofu,
    or 1 lb. reduced-fat, firm, regular tofu
1 c. reduced-fat soymilk
½ tsp. turmeric (optional)
¼ c. nutritional yeast flakes
1 green onion, chopped
¼ tsp. salt

Ranchero Sauce
1 medium onion, chopped
1 (14 oz.) can diced tomatoes, drained
½ c. juice from the canned tomatoes
2 T. pickled jalapeños, chopped
2 cloves garlic, minced
½ tsp. salt

4 corn tortillas, heated

To make the "omelets," preheat the oven to 400°F. Have ready two 9" lightly oiled or non-stick, metal pie pans. Blend the omelet ingredients together in a blender or food processor until very smooth. Divide the mixture evenly between the two prepared pans, and smooth the tops. Bake for 35 minutes.

Prepare the Ranchero Sauce as the omelets are baking. Steam-fry all the sauce ingredients together in a lightly oiled skillet until the onions are soft. Remove half of the sauce, and puree it in a blender or food processor. Pour the pureed mixture back into the skillet with the rest of the sauce, and keep warm until ready to serve.

To assemble the Tofu Rancheros, heat the tortillas by "dry-frying" them on a very hot, ungreased skillet (preferably cast iron) for a few seconds on each side, just until hot and slightly crispy. Divide the baked "omelets" in half, carefully loosen with a spatula, and place one half (folded, if necessary) on each heated tortilla. Top each serving with the Ranchero Sauce, and serve with Tofu Sour Cream and Vegetarian "Chorizo."

Serves 4

Per serving: Calories: 201, Protein: 18 gm., Fat: 3 gm., Carbohydrates: 26 gm.

Texas Caviar

Marinated Black-Eyed Pea Salad

Make this two or three days before serving, to intensify the flavors.

Bring the water to a boil in a heavy, medium-sized pot. Drop in the black-eyed peas, and boil for 2 minutes. Turn off the heat, cover, and let the peas soak for 1 hour. Now add the ½ tsp. salt, and bring the mixture to a boil again. Reduce the heat, cover, and simmer for 40 to 50 minutes, or until peas are tender but not mushy. Drain the peas in a colander, and discard the liquid. Place the peas in a serving bowl.

In a small saucepan, whisk the cornstarch into the cold water or broth, and stir constantly over high heat until the mixture has come to a boil. Stir and boil for 30 seconds.

Combine the cornstarch mixture with the vinegar, garlic, and remaining salt. Mix this dressing with the black-eyed peas, sliced onions, and parsley. Stir well, cover with plastic wrap, and marinate in the refrigerator for at least one day, preferably two or three. Stir the salad occasionally.

Before serving, taste for salt.

2½ c. water
1 c. dry black-eyed peas
½ tsp. salt

2 tsp. cornstarch
1 c. cold water or vegetarian broth

½ c. red wine vinegar
1 large garlic clove, crushed
1 tsp. salt

1 small onion, sliced
1 T. fresh parsley, minced

Serves 4 to 6

*Per serving: Calories: 107, Protein: 6 gm., Fat: 0 gm.,
Carbohydrates: 20 gm.*

Cranberry Sangria

*S*angria is a Spanish wine-and-fruit punch. In this non-alcoholic version, tangy cranberry juice cocktail takes the place of red wine, so that all age groups can enjoy it.

4 c. cranberry juice cocktail
1 lemon, thinly sliced
1 lime, thinly sliced
1 orange, thinly sliced
juice of 1 lemon or lime

2 c. seltzer water or sparkling lemon-
   lime drink
ice cubes
fresh fruit slices or chunks, for garnish
   (thread on bamboo skewers, if you
   wish, and use as stir-sticks)

Combine all of the ingredients except the seltzer water, ice cubes, and garnish in a punch bowl or serving pitcher. Refrigerate for at least one hour. Just before serving, add the seltzer, ice cubes, and fruit garnish.

Makes about 6 cups

Per cup: Calories: 113, Protein: 0 gm., Fat: 0 gm., Carbohydrates: 27 gm.

Mexican-Style Hot Chocolate

*M*exican hot chocolate is a rich concoction of frothy whipped milk, melted chocolate, and sugar, with a hint of almonds and cinnamon. Blending hot water, tofu, and cocoa powder (which gives the chocolate taste without the cocoa butter) results in a rich-tasting, frothy hot drink, minus the fat!

3 c. boiling water
½ (10.5 oz.) pkg. reduced-fat, firm or
   extra-firm, SILKEN tofu,
   or 8 oz. reduced-fat, firm or medium-
   firm, regular tofu
¼ c. sugar or alternate to taste
¼ c. unsweetened cocoa powder
1 tsp. pure vanilla extract
½ tsp. pure almond extract
¼ tsp. salt
¼ tsp. ground cinnamon

Mix all the ingredients in a blender until smooth and foamy. Pour into hot mugs and serve immediately.

For a mocha version, use hot coffee or coffee substitute instead of water.

Serves 4

Per serving: Calories: 83, Protein: 4 gm., Fat: 0 gm., Carbohydrates: 14 gm.

A Vietnamese Dinner Party

Most North Americans are aware of the Chinese New Year, especially those of us who live in large, coastal cities with a significant Chinese population. However, this holiday is also celebrated at the same time by another growing population in North America, the Vietnamese. The two-day holiday is called Tet in Vietnam, and, as in Chinese communities, there is much visiting back and forth, exchanging gifts of food and red envelopes of money for the children. Games of chance are played avidly, and there is an exciting display of fireworks. Vietnamese homes are traditionally adorned with peach blossoms, which represent peace and luck.

During the two days of celebration, no real cooking is done—snack foods (such as steamed rice cakes) and sweets are eaten. But on the day after the official celebration, there is usually a big family meal with traditional foods such as spring rolls.

I like to celebrate this holiday with the colorful, make-ahead Vietnamese meal that follows. Vietnamese food is light and flavorful, with very little fat and lavish use of fresh herbs and vegetables—just the thing to wake up sleepy palates as winter draws to a close. The Vietnamese like green teas, especially floral ones such as jasmine, but often end their meals with French-influenced Vietnamese coffee—a very strong, dripped coffee with sweetened condensed milk. Espresso with hot, sweetened soymilk (café au lait) would make a good vegan substitute.

Try to find a book on Chinese horoscopes so that your guests can find their Chinese/Vietnamese signs and predict their luck in the year ahead!

CHINESE/ VIETNAMESE NEW YEAR

Second New Moon after the
Winter Solstice

MENU

Baked Vietnamese Spring Rolls

Vietnamese Salad Rolls

Vietnamese Potato Patties

Vietnamese Cabbage Roll Soup

Braised Bean Curd

steamed long grain (jasmine) rice

Coconut Flan

café au lait

*beer, white wine, jasmine tea,
or carbonated water mixed with juice*

Look for rice papers, rice vermicelli noodles, and other Oriental foods in large supermarkets or Asian grocery stores, or check pages 186-87 for mail order sources. In place of the ubiquitous Vietnamese fish sauce, I use soy sauce—a light soy sauce is the best. If you miss that "fishy" taste, add a pinch or two of kelp powder along with the soy sauce.

Baked Vietnamese Spring Rolls

*T*hese crispy little tidbits are usually deep-fried, but you won't miss the grease! They are actually quite easy to make.

Have ready:

6 dried Chinese (shiitake) mushrooms, stemmed and soaked in hot water to cover for 30 minutes

1 oz. rice vermicelli noodles, soaked in hot water to cover for 30 minutes

1 recipe Vegetarian "Ground Pork," uncooked (p. 170)

24 (8½") round Vietnamese rice papers

2 qts. hot water in a large bowl with 1 c. sugar added

Dipping Sauce*

½ c. rice vinegar (or cider or white wine vinegar)

½ c. soy sauce

½ c. water

½ c. carrot, grated

¼ c. sugar, honey, or alternate sweetener

¼ c. lime juice

4 cloves garlic, pressed

2 T. pickled jalapeños, minced

---

*Vegetarian Nuoc Mam Sauce, which accompanies many Vietnamese dishes.

To make the Dipping Sauce, mix together all the dipping sauce ingredients in a small saucepan, and simmer briefly until the sugar is dissolved. Pour it into a bowl, and let it cool. This can be made well ahead of time and refrigerated, but let it come to room temperature before serving.

To make the filling, toss the slices of tofu with the 1 tablespoon soy sauce, and then dredge the slices in the yeast flakes, coating both sides. Cook the tofu in a heavy skillet, lightly greased (with Chinese sesame oil, if possible), over medium-high heat until both sides are golden-brown. Cut the tofu slices into very small dice.

In a large bowl, mix together the tofu, bean sprouts, carrot, onion, garlic, the whisked water-egg replacer mixture, mushrooms, vermicelli, and Vegetarian "Ground Pork." Combine well.

To fill the rolls, work with one rice paper at a time, and keep the rest covered. Spread out a clean, damp tea towel to cover your work surface. Dip a rice paper into the bowl of hot sugar-water for about 5 seconds, and smooth it out on the towel. The round should be pliable in a few seconds. Place 3 heaping tablespoons of filling on the bottom of the round. Shape the filling into a 4-inch "log" as neatly as you can. Fold the bottom up once, then fold the sides of the round over the filling and, starting at the filled end, roll it up into a tight cylinder. Place seam side down on a lightly oiled cookie sheet. Cover with a clean, damp towel or plastic wrap while you fill and roll the rest. (These can be made several hours before baking. Cover them tightly with plastic wrap, and refrigerate until baking time.)

To bake the rolls, preheat the oven to 400°F. Make sure that the rolls are at least 1" apart on the baking sheets. Brush the rolls lightly with the sugar-water, and bake them for 20-25 minutes, turning once half-way through. The rolls should be golden.

Cut each roll in half crosswise, on the diagonal (this is easiest with kitchen shears). Serve hot on a platter lined with lettuce leaves and decorated with grated carrot, fresh cilantro, and mint. Serve the dipping sauce alongside.

Makes 24 rolls

Per roll: Calories: 73, Protein: 7 gm., Fat: 1 gm., Carbohydrates: 10 gm.

Filling
6-7 oz. reduced-fat, extra-firm or
  pressed, regular tofu, sliced about
  ¼" thick
1 T. soy sauce

2 T. nutritional yeast flakes

1½ c. fresh mung bean sprouts,
  chopped,
  or green cabbage, thinly shredded
  and chopped
1½ c. carrot, grated
1 c. onion, minced
2 T. garlic, minced

6 T. water whisked together with:
¼ c. soy sauce
1½ T. powdered egg replacer
2 tsp. sugar or alternate sweetener
½ tsp. EACH salt and black pepper

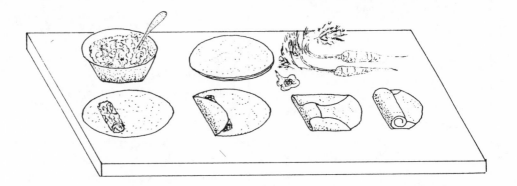

Vietnamese Salad Rolls

*Y*ou may have tasted these scrumptious rolls at a food fair or Vietnamese restaurant. They are actually very easy to make, and they can be made ahead of time, wrapped well with plastic wrap, and refrigerated until serving time. My version uses fresh herbs, of which the Vietnamese are very fond, so the rolls have a nice bite to them. I use a low-fat sauce based on Chinese hoisin sauce, which can be found in the Asian section of large supermarkets, instead of the usual peanut sauce.

Hoisin Dipping Sauce
1 small onion, minced and steam-fried until soft
6 T. water
1 T. + 1 tsp. Sesame Meal (p. 175)
1 T. + 1 tsp. miso
1 T. + 1 tsp. honey or other sweet syrup
½ tsp. rice or cider vinegar
¼ tsp. soy sauce
¼ tsp. Vietnamese or Thai chili paste
a few drops of peanut extract or flavoring (optional)

8 (8½") round Vietnamese rice papers

Filling
2 oz. rice vermicelli noodles

1 large carrot, scrubbed and shredded
1 tsp. sugar or alternate sweetener

8 medium lettuce leaves (your choice of variety), crisped
1 recipe Smoky Pan-Fried Tofu (p. 172), cut into slivers
1 c. fresh mung bean sprouts

Mix the ingredients for the Hoisin Dipping Sauce, and set aside.

To make the filling, soak the rice vermicelli in cold water to cover for 10-15 minutes. In the meantime, bring a pot of water to a boil. Remove the noodles from the cold water, and plunge them into the boiling water for 2 to 3 seconds. Drain the noodles in a colander, rinsing under cold running water. Set them aside in the colander.

Mix the carrots and sugar together in a small bowl.

Have a large bowl of warm water ready and a damp, clean towel on your work surface. Working with only 2 rice papers at a time (keep the rest covered), immerse each round in the warm water, quickly remove, and smooth them out on the towel. The rounds should be pliable within a few seconds.

To fill the rounds, lay one piece of lettuce over the bottom third of each round. On the lettuce, place ⅛ of the carrots, tofu, and bean sprouts, spreading out evenly so there won't be a bulge in the center. Roll this part toward the center once. Lay a green onion, 1 T. of the mint leaves, and 1 T. of the cilantro or basil leaves over the folded part, then roll the round up into a fairly tight cylinder. Place the rolls on a platter, and cover with a clean damp towel, then plastic wrap. Serve right away or refrigerate for several hours. Serve with the Hoisin Dipping Sauce to dip the rolls in as you eat.

Makes 8 large rolls

Per roll: Calories: 99, Protein: 7 gm., Fat: 1 gm., Carbohydrates: 17 gm.

8 small green onions, cut 8" long
½ c. fresh mint leaves*
½ c. fresh cilantro or basil*

*Fresh herbs are usually available year-round in produce sections of large supermarkets.

Vietnamese Potato Patties

These tasty morsels can be made ahead of time and frozen. Reheat them at 300°F for 30 minutes.

Squeeze the potatoes dry and place in a mixing bowl. Add the cornstarch and mix well. Add all of the remaining ingredients, and mix well again.

Heat two heavy, lightly oiled skillets over medium-high heat. Drop the mixture by table-spoons onto the skillets, forming them into 2½" patties. Cover the pans and cook until the bottoms of the patties are golden brown. Turn them over and cook, uncovered, until the other sides are golden brown and crispy.

Serve with the same Dipping Sauce as for the *Baked Vietnamese Spring Rolls* (see page 20).

Makes 30 patties

Per patty: Calories: 30, Protein: 0 gm., Fat: 0 gm., Carbohydrates: 7 gm.

4 medium russet potatoes, peeled, shredded, and soaked in cold water

½ c. cornstarch

1 T. powdered egg replacer beaten with ¼ c. water until frothy
1 medium onion, minced
4 green onions, minced
6 cloves garlic, minced
4 tsp. curry powder
2 tsp. soy sauce
black pepper to taste

Vietnamese Cabbage Roll Soup

*Y*ou can save yourself a lot of time and trouble if you freeze the cabbage for these cabbage rolls two days ahead of time. When they thaw out, the leaves will be limp and easily separated. The cabbage rolls can be made the day before the rest of the soup is made and refrigerated.

---

2 heads (about 2 lbs. each) savoy
    cabbage

2 oz. bean thread noodles or rice
    vermicelli noodles

Seasoning Sauce
¼ c. soy sauce
¼ c. water
4 cloves garlic, crushed
2 T. sugar or alternate sweetener
2 T. lime juice
¼ tsp. dried chili flakes

8 green onions

2½ quarts (10 c.) flavorful soy or
    vegetarian broth

Filling
1 recipe Vegetarian "Ground Pork,"
    uncooked (p. 170)
1 clove garlic, crushed
1 T. soy sauce
½ tsp. black pepper

At least 2 days before serving the soup, place the whole heads of savoy cabbage in plastic bags, and place in the freezer. Take them out of the freezer to thaw the night before making the soup.

The day you are serving the soup, soak the noodles in hot water to cover until soft, about 20 minutes; then drain and set aside.

Combine ingredients for the seasoning sauce, and set aside.

Cut the white bulbs off the green onions right up to where the stalks separate. Split each onion bulb in half lengthwise, trim the roots, and chop bulbs. Set chopped whites and intact green tops aside.

Remove and discard any bruised outer leaves of the thawed cabbages. Cut out and discard the cores. Separate the leaves and trim out any thick ribs. The pieces should be about 4" x 5". Cut large leaves in half to make this size, and use smaller leaves whole. Reserve under-sized leaves.

Start heating the broth in a large pot. When it boils, add the green onion tops, and cook for 30 seconds or until wilted. Remove them and drain. Cover the broth and keep it warm.

To make the filling, cut the noodles into 2" lengths, and mix with the Vegetarian "Ground Pork," garlic, soy sauce, black pepper, and ⅓ cup of the chopped green onion bulbs.

To fill the cabbage rolls, on the long side of each cabbage leaf, shape 1 tablespoon of filling into a "log" shape. Fold a long edge of the leaf over the filling, then fold the sides over the filling. Roll up tightly to make a neat package. Now tie a piece of green onion around the center of each roll, knotting it.

Bring the broth to boiling, and add the cabbage rolls. Simmer, uncovered, for 6 to 7 minutes. Lift the rolls out and place them on a platter.

Cut any extra cabbage leaves into ¼" strips, and add to the broth. Boil just until bright green, about 1 minute. Add soy sauce to taste, pour into a tureen or serving vessel, and sprinkle with the remaining chopped onion and the cilantro.

Place the rice in another bowl. To serve, fill each guest's bowl halfway with rice; spoon cabbage rolls and broth over the rice. Serve the seasoning sauce alongside.

Serves 6

Per serving: Calories: 395, Protein: 26 gm., Fat: 1 gm., Carbohydrates: 69 gm.

⅓ c. fresh cilantro, chopped

4 c. hot, steamed jasmine or other long grain rice

Vietnamese Braised Bean Curd
Tofu

*T*his is a simple but very tasty way to serve tofu.

---

3 (10.5 oz.) pkgs. reduced-fat, firm or
   extra-firm silken tofu,
   or 2 lbs. reduced-fat, firm or
   medium-firm, regular tofu

2 c. water or vegetarian broth
¼ c. Chinese brown bean sauce
2 T. sugar or alternate sweetener
½ tsp. black pepper

4 cloves garlic, minced

2 T. Sesame Meal (p. 175)

Preheat the oven to 400°F. Cut the tofu into ½" cubes, and cook in a nonstick skillet over medium heat until the cubes are golden brown on all sides.

Combine the water or vegetarian broth, bean sauce, sugar, and pepper in a small bowl, and set aside.

In a heavy skillet or wok lightly oiled with sesame oil, steam-fry the garlic over high heat for a few seconds. Add the sauce and the Sesame Meal, and bring to a boil. Add the tofu, cover, and simmer over low heat, stirring occasionally, for 20 minutes.

Serves 6 to 8

Per serving: Calories: 82, Protein: 10 gm., Fat: 2 gm., Carbohydrates: 4 gm.

Coconut Flan

*T*his light tofu pudding is very much like an egg custard made with coconut milk—a very common, Southeast Asian dessert. I like to serve it with chunks of canned pineapple and fresh mint sprigs as an edible decoration.

To make the syrup, bring the water and sugar to a boil over low heat in a small saucepan with a heavy bottom. Simmer, uncovered, for 5 minutes. Remove from the heat.

Working quickly, place the tofu, 2 tablespoons sugar, 1 tablespoon of syrup, the coconut extract, and salt in a blender. Set this aside and pour the remaining syrup evenly into 6 custard molds. Rotate each one to coat the base and sides with the syrup. Set aside.

Into the same saucepan, combine the nondairy milk and agar. Bring this quickly to a boil, stirring constantly, then reduce heat and simmer for 5 minutes. Continue stirring. Add this hot milk mixture to the ingredients in the blender, and immediately blend it into a smooth cream. Stir down the bubbles.

Pour the blended mixture into the coated molds, and skim off any remaining foam. Cover the molds with plastic wrap, and refrigerate them until serving time.

To unmold the puddings, dip the bottom of each mold briefly into boiling water, then remove the plastic wrap and turn upside down on a dessert plate. The pudding should slide out easily. Pour any syrup left in the bottom of the mold over the pudding.

Decorate each plate with fruit and mint or lemon balm sprigs.

Syrup
5 T. turbinado sugar or Sucanat
3 T. water

Pudding
⅔ c. reduced-fat, firm or medium-firm, regular tofu, crumbled
2 T. turbinado sugar or Sucanat
1 T. of the syrup, above
¾ tsp. coconut extract
pinch of salt

2½ c. reduced-fat soymilk or other non-dairy milk
1½ T. agar flakes, or ¾ tsp. agar powder

Serves 6

Per serving: Calories: 117, Protein: 4 gm., Fat: 2 gm., Carbohydrates: 21 gm.

VALENTINE'S DAY

February 14th

MENU

Sesame-Saffron Crêpes
with Artichoke Heart Stuffing
and Brandied Tomato Cream Sauce

Asparagus Salad
with
Carrot-Orange Dressing

Browned Onion Risotto

white wine
or
non-alcoholic white wine

Chocolate Hearts
or
Chocolate Cake Roll
with Sweet "Cream Cheese" Filling
and Raspberry Coulis (sauce)

espresso or coffee

A Romantic Dinner for Two

Valentine's Day is a day for lovers. It harkens back to the Ides of February in ancient Rome—the feast of Lupercalia—when young men chose small papers, or billets, with young women's names out of a large urn. The chosen couples would be sweethearts or erotic partners (depending on your source!) for the coming year. Since the early church could not eradicate this custom, it chose to Christianize it by making it the feast day of the apocryphal St. Valentine. Some Valentine's Day customs also recall those of the old Irish and English festivals of Brigid's Day/Candlemas or Beltane/May Day.

In Roman times and in the Middle Ages, people placed great stock in foods that were purported to have aphrodisiac qualities, and I thought it would be fun to include some of these (tomatoes or "love apples," onions, saffron, sesame, and chocolate) in our menu. Other traditional Valentine food associations which we have taken into consideration in our romantic dinner are the colors red and pink, creamy mixtures, heart-shaped cakes, and artichokes hearts.

So get out your best tableware, light the candles, put on some romantic mood music, and serve this dinner to your valentine. (It's much easier to make than it sounds!)

This menu could also be used for an anniversary, a small wedding supper, Candlemas, or May Day.

Asparagus Salad
with Carrot-Orange Vinaigrette

T his oil-free vinaigrette is fresh with the taste of orange juice.

Trim the tough ends off the asparagus. Steam the asparagus until it is bright green and tender but still crisp. Rinse it under cold water immediately, and drain well.

To make the vinaigrette, place the orange juice and cornstarch in a small pot, and stir over high heat until it is thickened and clear. Pour this into the blender with the other dressing ingredients, and blend until smooth. Pour this over the asparagus in a shallow glass dish, cover with plastic, and refrigerate for one hour.

Place 2 romaine lettuce leaves on each of four small plates. Remove the asparagus from the dressing, and divide it among the plates. Decorate with the shredded carrot and halved tomatoes, cover each plate with plastic wrap, and refrigerate until serving time. Serve the dressing on the side.

1-1¼ lbs. young, thin asparagus

Carrot-Orange Vinaigrette
¾ c. freshly-squeezed orange juice
1½ tsp. cornstarch
⅓ c. white wine vinegar
1 small carrot, scrubbed and diced
2 T. fresh parsley, chopped
1½ tsp. salt
1 clove garlic, peeled
¼ tsp. white pepper

8 large leaves romaine lettuce, washed and crisped
1 carrot, scrubbed and finely shredded
12 cherry tomatoes, stemmed and cut in half

Serves 4

Per serving: Calories: 97, Protein: 4 gm., Fat: 0 gm., Carbohydrates: 19 gm.

◆◇◆◇◆◇◆◇◆◇◆◇◆◇◆◇◆◇◆◇◆◇◆◇◆ ❤ ◇◆◇◆◇◆◇◆◇◆◇◆◇◆◇◆◇◆◇◆◇◆◇◆

Sesame-Saffron Crêpes

with Artichoke Heart Stuffing and Brandied Tomato Cream Sauce

You can use this crêpe recipe, minus the saffron and sesame meal, as a basic crêpe or French/Swedish/ English pancake recipe. For buckwheat crêpes (a specialty of Brittany), you can omit ½ cup of the unbleached flour, and substitute ½ cup buckwheat flour (these would be filled with steamed vegetables mixed with Tofu Sour Cream). Fill plain crêpes with any sweet or savory filling of your choice ("creamed" spinach, ratatouille, sweetened berries, asparagus, etc.) for limitless gourmet delicacies!

The crêpes, filling, and sauce can be prepared ahead of time, quickly assembled just before dinner, and heated for a few minutes before serving.

Place all of the crêpe ingredients in a blender, and blend until very smooth. Let stand for 30 minutes while you prepare the filling and sauce.

To prepare the stuffing, steam-fry the artichokes, mushrooms, green onions, and garlic in a large, lightly oiled skillet over high heat, using the wine as the liquid, until the mushrooms are cooked and the wine is almost all absorbed. Taste for salt and pepper. Set aside off the heat.

To prepare the sauce, whisk or blend all of the sauce ingredients together until smooth. Pour into a small, heavy saucepan, and bring to a boil over medium heat, stirring now and then. Turn heat to low and simmer gently for a few minutes. Remove from heat.

To make the crêpes, lightly oil an 8" crêpe pan or cast iron skillet with an oiled paper towel (or use a nonstick 8" skillet). Heat it over high heat until water sprinkled on it bounces off the

---

Crêpes
2 c. water
1 c. unbleached all-purpose flour
½ c. soy flour
2 T. nutritional yeast flakes
1 T. Sesame Meal (p. 175)
½ tsp. salt
¼ tsp. saffron (or 1 tsp. "American saffron" or dried marigold petals)

Artichoke Heart Stuffing
2 (14 oz.) cans artichoke hearts in water, drained and sliced,
   or 2 (9 oz.) pkgs. frozen artichoke hearts, thawed
8 large mushrooms, sliced (can be chanterelles, oyster mushrooms, fresh shiitakes or ordinary mushrooms)
8 green onions, chopped
4 large cloves garlic, minced (don't worry–you'll both smell like it! And, besides, garlic is supposed to be an aphrodisiac!)
1 c. dry white wine or non-alcoholic white wine
salt and black pepper to taste

surface.

Pour in about ¼ cup of the batter, and quickly rotate the pan until it evenly coats the bottom of the pan. When the crêpe starts to dry on the top, carefully but quickly loosen it with the underside of a metal spatula (pancake flipper), and turn it over. In a few seconds, remove it from the pan, and roll it up on a large plate. Continue with the remaining batter, oiling the pan lightly each time with the oiled paper towel. This batter is enough for 12 crêpes, but you might mess up a couple until you get the hang of it—that's okay!

To assemble the filled crêpes, preheat the oven to 400°F. Unroll the crêpes on a work surface, and divide the filling evenly among them, spooning the filling down the center of each crêpe. Roll them up and place them side by side in a shallow, lightly oiled baking pan. Bake them for about 10 minutes, or until the filling is hot. While they are baking, gently heat the sauce ingredients.

Serve the crêpes with some of the sauce poured over them.

Serves 4 (2 crêpes each)

Per crêpe: Calories: 148, Protein: 5 gm., Fat: 1 gm., Carbohydrates: 21 gm.

Brandied Tomato Cream Sauce
1⅓ c. water
1 (6 oz.) can good quality tomato paste
1 c. reduced-fat soymilk
¼ c. brandy (or non-alcoholic dry white wine, perhaps with a bit of brandy flavoring)
½ tsp. salt
½ tsp. dried thyme
¼ tsp. black pepper

Browned Onion Risotto

I used to think that risottos were too fatty and too time-consuming to have very often, until I discovered that you can make them easily with almost no fat and very little effort! I often can't find Italian arborio rice in my area, so I substitute a short grain rice instead, with good results.

2 large onions, thinly sliced
2 cloves garlic, minced

1⅓ c. arborio or short grain rice
2½ c. vegetarian broth
⅔ c. dry white wine or non-alcoholic
    white wine
1 tsp. dried rosemary
½ tsp. salt

white pepper to taste

In a lightly oiled, heavy pot, steam-fry the onion until soft and nicely browned. Add the garlic toward the end of the cooking time. Add the remaining ingredients, except the pepper, and bring to a boil. Reduce the heat to low, and simmer, uncovered, until thick and creamy, stirring now and then for about 30 minutes. If there's not enough liquid at the end, add a tiny bit of water at a time. Add white pepper to taste.

If you like, add ¼-½ cup soy parmesan.

Serves 4

Per serving: Calories: 248, Protein: 5 gm., Fat: 0 gm., Carbohydrates: 48 gm.

Chocolate Hearts or Roll

with
Sweet "Cream Cheese"
Filling and Raspberry Coulis

Y ou'll never believe that a chocolate cake with 1 or less grams of fat per slice can taste so rich—until you try it! (By the way, "coulis" is just the French word for a fruit or vegetable puree or sauce.)

To make the cake batter, preheat the oven to 350°F. Follow the directions for making the batter for the chocolate variation of the *Basic Holiday Cake Roll*.

To make Chocolate Hearts, scrape the batter evenly into 12 lightly oiled or nonstick, heart-shaped muffin cups. Bake for 20-25 minutes at 350°F, or until they test done. Do not overbake. Carefully remove from pans and cool on racks.

To make a Chocolate Roll, follow the directions for baking, rolling, and cooling the *Basic Holiday Cake Roll*, using unsweetened cocoa instead of powdered sugar when rolling.

To fill the Chocolate Hearts, slice them in half horizontally with a serrated knife, using a careful sawing motion. Spread some of the filling on each bottom half, then place the top half over that. Refrigerate, well covered with plastic wrap, until serving time.

To fill the Chocolate Roll, follow the directions for filling, rolling, and refrigerating the *Basic Holiday Cake Roll*. Just before serving, carefully cut the roll into 12 slices with a serrated knife, using a gentle sawing motion.

(cont.)

Basic Holiday Cake Roll, chocolate
   variation (p. 154-55)
Sweet "Cream Cheese" Filling from
   Holiday Cake Roll (p. 154)

Raspberry Coulis
2 c. frozen unsweetened raspberries,
   thawed*
sweetener to taste (¼-½ c. sugar)
2 tsp. cornstarch or other starch,
   dissolved in 1 T. water

*Strawberries can be used in place of
   raspberries

To make the Coulis, puree the raspberries in a food processor or blender until smooth. Pour into a medium saucepan, and stir over high heat until quite hot. Add sweetener of your choice until it tastes right to you. Stir until it is dissolved. Stir in the dissolved cornstarch, and continue stirring over high heat until the sauce has thickened. Refrigerate until serving time.

For each serving, place two hearts or two slices of cake roll on a pool of coulis on each dessert plate, and pass the remaining coulis at the table. (If you like, the slices of cake roll can be placed together and formed to make a heart shape.) Unfilled cupcakes can be frozen. Filled cake keeps well for several days in the refrigerator, well-wrapped.

Serves 6

Per serving: Calories: 356, Protein: 12 gm., Fat: 2 gm., Carbohydrates: 72 gm.

BUFFET OF INDIAN SNACK FOODS

One of the most colorful Hindu holidays in India is called Holi, celebrating Lord Krishna's victory over the evil ogress, Holika. Holi is celebrated most uproariously (with exploding fireworks and everyone throwing colored water and colored powders at one another) in Northern India and in Bengal. A carnival mood prevails, with crowds dressed in their newly-cleaned clothes, singing love songs around bonfires, watching performers enact episodes from Krishna's life, and eating spicy delicacies from street vendors.

Most popular are wadas (sometimes spelled vadas or badas)—patties made from ground, soaked legumes mixed with spices and vegetables and sometimes some sort of starch or grain. Wadas are traditionally deep-fried, but here we bake them. The results are not as crispy, but still quite delicious.

The following menu is not a proper Indian dinner—in the spirit of Holi it consists of various Indian snack foods and desserts, revised to lower the fat content drastically while losing none of the mouth-watering goodness that makes "street food" so irresistible.

This could also be a spring equinox buffet.

HOLI
(India's Spring Festival)
Full Moon,
February-March

MENU

*Baked Samosas
with Two Fillings*

Aloo Tikki

Pan-roasted Poppadoms

Tandoori Kebabs

beer, tea, or juice

Wadas

several chutnies

sliced, raw vegetables

*chapathis
or
whole wheat pita bread*

Tofu "Yogurt" (p. 174)

Shrikand

fresh fruit

Lassi

Baked Samosas
Savory Indian Stuffed Pastries

L ike most Indian snack foods or appetizers, these crispy pastries are usually deep-fried, but phyllo (or filo) pastry, available frozen in most supermarkets, makes a fine (and much easier!) substitute for fried dough. These will disappear in minutes! NOTE: You can make ½ a recipe of each filling and make some of each kind; or make just one filling.

Have ready:
9 full sheets of phyllo pastry, thawed
    and kept covered
soymilk for brushing tops

Vegetable Filling
½ lb. thin-skinned potatoes
2 medium onions, minced
1 T. ground coriander
½ tsp. ground cumin
¼ tsp. cayenne pepper
10 oz. frozen peas, thawed and drained
⅓ c. fresh cilantro or parsley, chopped
salt to taste

"Meat" Filling
1½ c. dry textured vegetable protein
    granules
1 c. plus 2 T. boiling water
2 T. soy sauce
4 medium onions, minced
2 cloves garlic, minced
4 tsp. curry powder
2 tsp. fresh ginger, minced
2 tsp. garam masala
1 tsp. salt
2 T. lemon juice
4 T. fresh cilantro, mint or parsley,
    chopped (or 4 tsp. dried)

To make the vegetable filling, cook the potatoes in boiling water until tender but not mushy (cut larger potatoes into big chunks). Drain and cut them into ½" cubes. Set aside to cool.

In a large, lightly oiled or nonstick skillet, steam-fry the onions until they are limp. Add the coriander, cumin, and cayenne, and stir-fry for one minute. Remove from the heat and add the cubed potatoes, thawed peas, and cilantro or parsley. Mix well and taste for salt. Allow to cool.

To make the textured vegetable protein "meat" filling, first reconstitute the granules in the boiling water with the soy sauce in a small bowl. Steam-fry the onions and garlic in a heavy, lightly oiled or nonstick skillet until limp. Add the curry powder, ginger, garam masala, and salt, and stir-fry for one minute. Add the vegetable protein, the cilantro or mint, and lemon juice. Mix well and allow to cool.

To fill the samosas, stack 3 sheets of phyllo together, and cut into four 6" x 5" rectangles. Repeat with the remaining phyllo. You should have 36 rectangles. Keep the phyllo well covered with plastic wrap while you work.

For each samosa, place 3 tablespoons of filling in one corner of a rectangle of phyllo. Roll the filled end toward the center, then fold in the left and right corners (like an envelope), then roll up again. Cover the filled samosas with plastic wrap while you fill the others.

Preheat the oven to 400°F. Place the filled samosas, seam side down, on lightly oiled cookie sheets. Brush the tops with soymilk. Bake the samosas for about 20 minutes, or until golden brown. Serve the samosas hot with chutney.

Makes 36 samosas

Per samosa: Calories: 44, Protein: 3 gm., Fat: 0 gm., Carbohydrates: 8 gm.

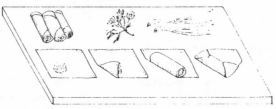

Aloo Tikki
Indian-Style Potato Cakes

This is a delectable way to serve the common potato. The traditional way is to mix the potatoes with panir, a homemade Indian curd cheese. But here we substitute mashed, firm tofu, with excellent results.

Mix all of the ingredients in a medium bowl, mashing well with your fingers. Heat a couple of heavy, lightly oiled skillets over medium-low heat. With wet hands, form the mixture into 20 to 24 patties. (If the mixture is too loose, add a few tablespoons of chickpea flour.) Cook the patties until nicely browned on the bottom, then turn them over and brown the other side. Repeat with any remaining patties. Serve the patties hot with chutney.

Makes 20 to 24 patties

Per patty: Calories: 29, Protein: 1 gm., Fat: 0 gm., Carbohydrates: 5 gm.

3 c. boiled russet potatoes, mashed (with no milk or seasoning)
1 c. reduced-fat, firm, regular tofu, mashed
3 T. fresh cilantro or parsley, chopped
3 T. pickled jalapeños, chopped
1 T. lemon juice
2 tsp. fresh ginger, minced
1-2 tsp. salt, to taste
¼ tsp. turmeric

Pan-Roasted Poppadoms

You may have been served these crunchy lentil wafers before an Indian meal in a restaurant. They are popular all over India. They are nutritious and fat-free if roasted on a dry pan instead of deep-fried.

Poppadoms are available in Indian grocery stores and many large supermarkets and health food stores. The plain or cumin ones are good with salsa and other spicy dips. The red pepper, black pepper, green chili, and garlic varieties are good with Tofu Sour Cream or "Yogurt" (see p. 174) and chutney.

I often take about 15 minutes to cook up a whole package of poppadoms at once, and then store the crisp, cooled wafers in a rigid plastic container for weeks. They make a delicious, fat-free (and inexpensive) substitute for tortilla chips and potato chips.

Heat a heavy (preferably cast iron), dry skillet (ungreased) over high heat. Have a pair of cooking tongs handy. When the pan is hot, place a poppadom on it. In a few seconds, it will turn lighter in color, and tiny bubbles will appear all over the surface. Turn it over with the tongs (there may be a few scorched spots, but that's all right), and cook the other side for a few seconds, until the whole poppadom is a lighter color. Quickly remove it to a plate, rack, or dry counter to cool, and cook the rest, working very quickly. The poppadoms seem limp at first, but get crispy immediately upon cooling.

To microwave, line the carousel of a large microwave oven with paper towels. Place 3 poppadoms on it, not touching. Mirowave on HIGH for 1½ minutes.

Tandoori Kebabs

*T*hese scrumptious kebabs can be made easily in your oven broiler at any time of the year, or on a hibachi, indoor grill, or barbecue.

Cut the tofu into 48 equal cubes, and marinate *at least* 12 hours in Breast of Tofu Marinade.

In a shallow glass or plastic container or dish, mix together the Tandoori Marinade ingredients, and add the tofu cubes, mixing well and making sure the tofu cubes are covered. Cover and marinate for several hours, or refrigerate for several days.

Thread the tofu cubes and mushroom caps alternately on the skewers (6 tofu cubes and 4 mushrooms per skewer). Broil, grill, or barbecue the skewers, basting with the marinade occasionally, until slightly charred on two sides. Serve hot in chapathis, whole wheat pita bread, or flour tortillas, heated briefly, with Tofu Sour Cream or "Yogurt," chutney, and perhaps sliced raw vegetables on the side, to eat like a pita sandwich (with lots of napkins!).

Instead of the tofu, or alternating with the tofu, you can also use reconstituted textured vegetable protein chunks (see p. 169), lightly-seasoned seitan chunks, or chunks of rinsed, canned Chinese "Vegetarian Roast Duck" (called Mun Chai Ya, a gluten product). Marinate all in the Tandoori Marinade.

Makes 8 skewers

Per skewer: Calories: 106, Protein: 11 gm., Fat: 3 gm., Carbohydrates: 10 gm.

---

1 (14 oz.) pkg. reduced-fat, extra-firm or pressed, regular tofu
1 recipe Breast of Tofu Marinade (p. 172)

Tandoori Marinade
1 c. Tofu "Yogurt" (p. 174)
2 medium onions, diced
4 tsp. ground ginger
2 tsp. turmeric
1 tsp. curry powder
1 tsp. chile powder
½ tsp. EACH ground coriander, cumin, garlic granules, nutmeg, and paprika

32 small mushroom caps
8 bamboo skewers, soaked in cold water for at least 15 minutes

Wadas

Savory Split Pea Patties

This is a somewhat unorthodox recipe for wadas—an oven-baked version. They are at their best when just taken out of the oven, but I've even munched them cold out of the refrigerator and been surprised at how tasty they are! NOTE: You need a food processor for this recipe.

1 c. yellow split peas
2 T. pickled jalapeños, chopped
½ tsp. dried red chile flakes

⅓ c. onion, minced
2 T. fresh ginger, minced
2 T. fresh cilantro, minced
1½ tsp. salt

1 c. steam-fried cabbage, chopped
   (2 c. raw)
1 tsp. baking powder

Rinse and soak the split peas for at least 4 hours in enough water to cover. Drain, rinse, and drain again. Place them in a food processor along with the jalapeños, chile flakes, and 3 tablespoons water. Add the onion, ginger, cilantro, and salt, and process until smooth. Add the cabbage and baking powder, and process again. Place the batter in a bowl and refrigerate—the patties are easier to form when cold.

Preheat the oven to 450°F. With wet hands, form the batter into 24 ¼"-thick patties, and place on 2 oiled cookie sheets. Bake for 5 minutes on each side.

Serve hot with Tofu "Yogurt" (p. 174) and chutney.

Makes 40 patties

Per patty: Calories: 26, Protein: 2 gm., Fat: 0 gm., Carbohydrates: 5 gm.

Shrikand
Gujarati "Yogurt" Pudding

This aromatic, sweet pudding from Gujarat in India is usually made with thick, whole-milk yogurt which is hung to drain. It is very rich. Extra-firm, silken tofu makes a surprisingly rich-tasting substitute—this version is delicious, sweet with a nice tang to it.

Mix all of the ingredients in a food processor until very smooth. Spoon into 6 pudding dishes (as decorative as possible), cover with plastic wrap, and chill for *at least* 2 hours.

Serves 6

Per serving: Calories: 101, Protein: 7 gm., Fat: 1 gm., Carbohydrates: 16 gm.

---

2 (10.5 oz.) pkgs. reduced-fat, extra-firm, SILKEN tofu
⅓ c. honey,
    or ½ c. powdered sugar
¼ c. lemon juice
¼ tsp. salt
¼ tsp. pure almond extract
¼ tsp. saffron
¼ tsp. EACH ground nutmeg and cardamom

Lassi

Indian "Yogurt" and Fruit Drink

Lassi can be sweet or savory, but it is always refreshing. Traditionally made with yogurt or buttermilk, it can be made with tofu and lemon juice so successfully that no one will know the difference. This makes a great snack or dessert anytime, and many combinations of flavors are possible.

Fruit (use ONE of the following):
1⅓ c. ripe peeled mango, papaya, or
    pineapple, chopped,
or 1 c. frozen peach cocktail concen-
    trate, pineapple or papaya juice
    concentrate,
or 1 c. apricot nectar or Fruit Nectar*

Liquid (use ONE of the following):
2⅔ c. cold water + ¼ c. honey or
    alternate sweetener,
or 2 c. cold water + ⅔ c. frozen apple
    juice concentrate,
or 3 c. fruit juice of choice

Additional Ingredients
1 c. reduced-fat, medium-firm, regular
    or SILKEN tofu
12 ice cubes
¼ c. lemon juice

Optional Ingredients
2 tsp. dairy-free acidophilus powder
½ tsp. coconut extract OR ground
    cardamom, nutmeg or ginger

Place the fruit of your choice, liquid of your choice, additional ingredients, and any optional ingredients in the blender container. (Make sure that your blender can take ice cubes without damaging it.) Blend until the ice is well ground up and the mixture is frothy. Pour into glasses and serve immediately.

*Fruit Nectar to use in Lassi: Soak ½ cup dried apricots, peaches, or papayas in 2 cups pineapple juice until soft. Whiz in a blender until smooth. Use this in place of canned apricot nectar or frozen juice concentrate when fresh fruit is not available.

Serves 6 to 8

Per serving: Calories: 94, Protein: 4 gm., Fat: 2 gm., Carbohydrates: 16 gm.

An Irish Farmhouse Dinner

In North America, we are used to celebrating St. Patrick's Day in a rather gaudy and raucous fashion, with parades, paper shamrocks draping everything in sight, and nauseating offers of everything from green beer to green bread!

In their native country, however, the Irish celebrate their patron saint's day as a religious holiday, with most people attending church services.

We might take this opportunity to celebrate the wonderful simplicity and freshness of traditional Irish cookery on this day, with a menu that features not only the ubiquitous potato, but the fresh produce (particularly greens), hot quick breads, and apples of the Emerald Isle.

This menu could also be used for a Sabbath meal (everything can be made ahead), Father's Day, Lammas, or Halloween. For Lammas, or Lughnasa, the Irish First Fruits Festival, use raw berries instead of the poached apples in the pudding. On Halloween, it is an old tradition to hide trinkets in the colcannon which tell fortunes for the following year for those who find them in their portion. The trinkets might be a coin for wealth, a ring for a bride, etc. (Please warn your guests if you do this, so that no one chokes on a trinket!)

ST. PATRICK'S DAY
March 17

MENU

Vegetarian Irish Stew
with Guiness Stout

Herbed Oatmeal Oven Scones

Colcannon
(mashed potatoes with cabbage or kale)

Irish Apple Bread Pudding

beer, stout, or tea

Irish coffee (optional)

Vegetarian Irish Stew
with Guiness Stout

T his stew is entirely my own invention and contains such non-Irish ingredients as soy sauce and red lentils. But it has the taste and texture of a good brown stew (or "gypsy," as it's called in some Irish homes), and it's delicious served with colcannon.

If you don't want to use alcohol (even though most of it cooks off during the simmering), use the darkest non-alcoholic beer you can find instead of the Guiness Stout (an Irish product that can be found in most liquor stores).

2 medium onions, sliced
¼ c. unbleached flour
4 c. water
1 c. Guiness Stout (or dark, non-alcoholic beer)
2 c. mushrooms, thickly sliced
1 c. carrot or parsnips, sliced into rounds
1 c. turnips or rutabagas, peeled and in large dice
1 c. celery, diced
½ c. split red lentils
½ c. fresh parsley, chopped
¼ c. soy sauce or mushroom soy sauce
3 vegetarian or soy bouillon cubes
1 bay leaf
2 tsp. Marmite or other yeast extract
1 tsp. sugar or alternate sweetener
¼ tsp. EACH dried thyme, rosemary, and marjoram
black pepper to taste
a dash of Kitchen Bouquet for color (optional)
1 c. dry textured vegetable protein chunks (p. 169) (optional)

In a large, lightly oiled, heavy pot, steam-fry the onion until it begins to soften. Add the flour and stir around thoroughly. Add the remaining ingredients, mix well, and bring to a boil. Cover, turn down to low, and simmer for about 30 minutes, or until the vegetables are done. Taste for seasoning. Serve with Colcannon on the facing page.

Serves 6

Per serving: Calories: 114, Protein: 5 gm., Fat: 0 gm., Carbohydrates: 22 gm.

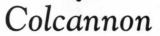

Colcannon
Mashed Potatoes with Kale or Cabbage

There are many versions of this dish—with peas instead of cabbage or kale, it's called "Champ" in Ireland; in Scotland it's sometimes called "Rumbledethumps" when made with cabbage, "Tatties'n'Neeps" when made with mashed turnips and chives, and "Clapshot" when made with mashed rutabagas! The Dutch version of colcannon is called "Stampot." It's delicious by any name, especially when served with the gravy from the vegetarian stew above, instead of the usual melted butter.

Cut the potatoes into chunks, and boil in water to cover until tender, but not mushy.

Meanwhile, wash and trim the kale or cabbage, discarding any tough stems. Chop it and steam for 5-10 minutes, or until tender. Cool it and gently squeeze out the water. At the same time, in a lightly oiled skillet, steam-fry the leeks until softened.

Drain the potatoes well and mash with a potato masher. Beat in the soymilk, then the cooked kale or cabbage and leeks. Add salt and pepper to taste. Serve hot with stew or gravy.

Serves 6

Per serving: Calories: 285, Protein: 7 gm., Fat: 1 gm., Carbohydrates: 61 gm.

---

3 lbs. russet potatoes, peeled

2 lbs. kale or green or Savoy cabbage
2 c. leeks or green onions, minced
¾ c. soy or other non-dairy milk
salt and black pepper to taste

Herbed Oatmeal Oven Scones

G riddle breads are scones that are cooked on a griddle on top of the stove. This was the primary method of cooking scones in Ireland, Scotland, and Wales for centuries. Modern cooks have ovens, but often not a heavy griddle or the patience to keep a watchful eye so that the breads cook evenly, so these small breads (called scones for want of a better description, though they are not sweet) are oven-baked. They are moist and delicious, even without the modern addition of shortening.

---

1 c. rolled oats
1¼ c. reduced-fat soymilk mixed with
   1 T. lemon juice or vinegar
½ c. fresh herbs of your own choosing,
   chopped and loosely-packed (parsley, chives, savory, sage, thyme,
   rosemary, etc.)

1¼ c. unbleached flour
1 tsp. sugar or alternate sweetener
½ tsp. baking soda
½ tsp. salt

caraway seeds for sprinkling on top
   (optional)

Variations

For a sweet scone, omit the herbs and sprinkle the tops with sugar before baking. You can also add ¼ cup dried currants or other dried fruit, if you like.

For Currant-Apple Scones, omit the herbs, use 3 tablespoons sugar in the dough, and add ½ cup dried currants and ¾ cup grated apple. Sprinkle the tops of the scones with sugar before baking.

Preheat the oven to 400°F.

Place the rolled oats in a DRY blender or food processor, and whirl until the oats are ground to a fine meal. Pour them into a small bowl, and stir in the soymilk mixture. Add the fresh herbs.

In a medium bowl, mix the flour, sugar, baking soda, and salt. Pour in the oat mixture, and mix briefly with a fork. Divide the dough in two. With wet hands, pat each half of the dough into an 8" circle in a lightly oiled or nonstick 9" cake pan. Score each circle into 6 wedges. If you like, sprinkle the tops with caraway seeds. Bake for 15-20 minutes, or until golden, and serve hot.

Served as an accompaniment to the stew, these wedges can be dunked in the gravy. Served for tea or breakfast, you can omit the herbs, split them with a fork, and spread them with jam or marmalade.

Makes 12 scones

Per scone: Calories: 80, Protein: 3 gm., Fat: 0 gm., Carbohydrates: 15 gm.

Irish Apple Bread Pudding

*I*n researching the cooking of Ireland, I've noticed that apple desserts take pride of place. This homey but delectable dessert perfectly complements our vegan "farmhouse" dinner.

Poach the apples for 10 minutes in the apple juice.

In a lightly oiled, 9" square pan, place 4 slices of bread, cut to fit the bottom of the pan. Place the poached apples and the currants or raisins over the bread. Top with the remaining bread.

In a medium bowl, whisk together the soymilk, sugar, nutritional yeast, cinnamon, vanilla, and salt. Pour over the bread and apples. Let sit for 20 minutes while you preheat the oven to 375°F.

Sprinkle the top of the pudding with nutmeg. Place the pan inside of a larger one with hot water in the bottom. Bake for 30 minutes.

To make the Brown Sugar Sauce, mix together all of the sauce ingredients *except* the vanilla or whiskey in a small saucepan. Bring to a boil, stirring, and simmer 5 minutes. Stir in the vanilla or whiskey. (If you want the whiskey flavor without the alcohol, add the whiskey at the beginning of the cooking time, so that the alcohol boils off.) Serve warm over the hot bread pudding.

4 small apples (about 1 lb.), cored and sliced (peel only if the skins are unsightly or sprayed)
¼ c. apple juice

8 thin slices of bread (not a heavy bread), hard crusts removed
2 T. dried currants or raisins

1¾ c. reduced-fat soymilk
⅓ c. sugar or Sucanat
1½ T. nutritional yeast flakes
1 tsp. ground cinnamon
1 tsp. pure vanilla extract
¼ tsp. salt
sprinkle of ground nutmeg

Brown Sugar Sauce
1 c. water
½ c. brown sugar or Sucanat
1 T. cornstarch
1 T. pure vanilla extract or a liquor extract,
   or 3 T. Irish whiskey
pinch of salt

Serves 6

Per serving: Calories: 220, Protein: 5 gm., Fat: 1 gm., Carbohydrates: 47 gm.

NAW RUZ
(Baha'i New Year)
Spring Equinox

MENU

Green Hummus
with pita bread

Sambusak
(stuffed pastries)

Potato and Pickle Salad

Tabbouleh
(bulgur wheat and parsley salad)

Persian Stuffed Peppers

Iranian Orange Drink

Orange and Lemon Semolina Pudding

fresh fruit in season

❖❖❖❖❖❖❖❖❖❖❖❖❖❖❖❖❖❖❖❖❖

Persian-Israeli Naw Ruz Buffet Dinner

The original Naw Ruz predates Islam, but is now celebrated primarily by the Baha'i Faith, one of the fastest-growing religious communities in the world. The Baha'i religion originated in Iran, but Baha'is were persecuted there and now are dispersed worldwide, with their headquarters in Israel.

After a 19-day fast, during which healthy individuals over the age of 15 are expected to refrain from food and drink from sunrise to sunset, families and friends gather together on the day of the vernal (spring) equinox to feast and celebrate. As with most other spring holidays, it is a time of spiritual growth and renewal.

In honor of the countries where the Baha'i Faith came into being and now has its center, we are presenting a vegetarian, Persian-Israeli buffet dinner. Everything can be made ahead and either served cold or reheated.

This menu would also make an excellent spring equinox or spring wedding dinner.

Green Hummus

Most versions of this popular Middle Eastern chickpea dip are chock-full of olive oil and sesame tahini, but just a little Sesame Meal adds flavor with a fraction of the fat. Spinach highlights the Persian fondness for greens, and it's a delicious touch! Serve with wedges of whole wheat pita bread.

Place all of the ingredients *except* the spinach in the food processor. Process until it is as smooth as you like it, adding a bit of water or chickpea broth if necessary (it thickens up in the refrigerator). Add the spinach and process again briefly. Place in a serving bowl, cover with plastic wrap, and refrigerate until serving time.

Makes about 3½ cups

Per ¼ cup serving: Calories: 52, Protein: 2 gm., Fat: 0 gm., Carbohydrates: 8 gm.

2 c. well-cooked or canned chickpeas, drained
⅓ c. lemon juice
2 T. Sesame Meal (p. 175)
6 cloves garlic, peeled
1½ tsp. salt
1 tsp. ground cumin
¼ tsp. cayenne pepper

1 (10 oz.) pkg. frozen chopped spinach, thawed and squeezed dry

Plain Hummus

Omit the spinach and decrease the salt to 1 tsp., the cumin to ½ tsp., and the cayenne to a pinch.

Persian Stuffed Peppers

Persians use many vegetables for stuffing, so if you prefer, use 8 large tomatoes, instead of the peppers, with the stem end sliced off and the insides scooped out (use the chopped pulp in the filling), or any other vegetable of your choice.

1 large onion, chopped and steam-fried
   until soft
½ c. tomato sauce
juice and grated peel of 1 lemon
pinch of sugar
salt and black pepper to taste

1 c. basmati rice
1½ c. vegetarian broth

½ recipe Vegetarian "Burger", cooked
   and crumbled (p. 171)
1 c. fresh parsley, chopped
1 c. green onions, chopped
2 T. dried dillweed
1 tsp. dried tarragon, crushed
1 tsp. dried mint, crushed

8 medium red or green bell peppers

½ c. tomato sauce
1 c. vegetarian broth

In a large, lightly oiled skillet with a tight lid, mix the steam-fried onions with the ½ cup tomato sauce, lemon juice and peel, sugar, and salt and pepper to taste. Add the rice and stir over high heat for a few minutes. Add the 1½ cup broth, and bring to a boil. Reduce the heat, cover, and simmer 10-15 minutes, or until the liquid is almost all absorbed. Stir in the "burger," parsley, green onions, dill, tarragon, and mint; cover and cook 5 more minutes. Preheat the oven to 350°F.

Cut the tops off the peppers, and remove the seeds and membrane from the tops and the bottoms of the peppers. Spoon equal amounts of the rice filling into all of the peppers, and place them standing up in a shallow baking dish. Mix together the last ½ cup tomato sauce and 1 cup broth, and pour around the peppers. Cover the peppers with their own tops, and cover the baking pan with foil. Bake 1 hour, or until the peppers are tender. This can be served hot or at room temperature.

Makes 8 stuffed peppers

Per pepper: Calories: 139, Protein: 9 gm., Fat: 1 gm., Carbohydrates: 23 gm.

Sambusak
Stuffed Pastries

Stuffed pastries of many kinds are popular in the Middle East—sambusaks are much loved by Sephardic and Persian Jews. In this version, we replace the rich yeast dough with our soft, versatile, yeasted pastry dough, and the deep-frying with baking.

You have a choice of a "meaty" filling made with our homemade Vegetarian "Burger," or a tasty Swiss chard and tofu "feta" filling, quite similar to a Greek spanikopita (spinach pie) filling. (If you can't decide, double the dough recipe and make both, or cut the filling recipes in half, and make 12 of each!) You might like to experiment later with other fillings of your own invention, such as mushroom or eggplant mixtures with Middle Eastern seasonings.

To make the "meat" filling, in a lightly oiled, heavy skillet, steam-fry the green onions, garlic, and ginger for a few minutes. Add the cinnamon and turmeric, and stir-fry for a few seconds. Add the crumbled Vegetarian "Burger," and mix well. (Add any options, if using.) Taste for seasoning and cool thoroughly.

To make the chard and "feta" filling, mix all the ingredients together thoroughly.

Optional additions with either filling could be leftover cooked peas and/or diced potatoes, ordinary onion, chopped green pepper, parsley, a pinch of ground cloves and nutmeg, or a bit of ground cumin.

To make the sambusak, cut the risen dough into 24 equal pieces, and cover the ones you aren't working with. Roll each piece into a ball, then, on a lightly floured surface, roll each ball into a ¼"-thick circle. Place a mounded table-spoon of filling in the center (you can divide the filling up equally into 24 portions beforehand, if you like). Run a finger which has been dipped in water around the inside edge of the dough.

(cont.)

1 recipe Yeasted Pastry Dough (p. 144),
    with 2 tsp. ground anise seed added

"Meat" Filling
1 bunch green onions, chopped
1 clove garlic, crushed
1 tsp. fresh ginger, minced
1 tsp. ground cinnamon
¼ tsp. turmeric
1 recipe Vegetarian "Burger", cooked
    and crumbled (p. 171)
salt and black pepper to taste

Chard and "Feta" Filling
2 lbs. Swiss chard, spinach or other
    greens, chopped, steamed and
    drained dry
1½ lbs. medium-firm, regular tofu,
    drained and crumbled
1 large onion, minced and steam-fried
¼ c. light miso
2 T. nutritional yeast flakes
2 T. fresh parsley, minced
1 tsp. salt
½ tsp. ground nutmeg
½ tsp. black pepper

Starch Glaze (p. 142)
2 T. sesame seeds for garnish

Makes about 24 pastries

Per pastry with "meat" filling: Calories: 155, Protein: 9 gm., Fat: 1 gm., Carbohydrates: 28 gm.

Per pastry with chard and "feta" filling: Calories: 179, Protein: 8 gm., Fat: 1 gm., Carbohydrates: 32 gm.

Fold one side of the dough over to the other side to make a half-moon or turnover shape. Seal the edges with fork tines. Place the filled sambusak, not touching, on lightly oiled cookie sheets, and keep covered until all are filled. Preheat the oven to 350°F.

Brush the sambusak with Starch Glaze, and sprinkle the tops with sesame seeds. Bake until golden brown (do not rise first), about 15 minutes. Serve hot or reheat later. These can be successfully frozen.

Persian Potato and Pickle Salad
Salad-e Khiar Shur

4 medium carrots, cooked or pickled, diced
1½-2 c. cooked or canned red kidney beans or small red beans, drained
2 large red-skinned potatoes, freshly cooked and diced
2 large dill pickles, chopped
10 radishes, sliced
1 bunch green onions, chopped
1 bunch parsley, minced
¼ c. fresh mint, chopped (or 2 T. dried)
½ small head of green cabbage, cored and shredded (optional)

Dressing
¾ c. cold vegetarian broth
2 tsp. cornstarch
½ c. lemon juice
1-2 cloves garlic, crushed
1 tsp. salt
1 tsp. dried tarragon
½ tsp. white pepper

This colorful salad is perfect for any holiday buffet.

Assemble all of the salad ingredients in a large bowl. Stir the cornstarch and broth in a small saucepan over high heat until it boils and thickens. Whisk this with the other dressing ingredients, and pour over the salad. Toss well and add salt to taste.

If you prefer a creamy dressing, add ½ cup Tofu Sour Cream (p. 174) or tofu mayonnaise (p. 174) or store-bought.

Refrigerate for at least one hour, or overnight.

Serves 8

Per serving: Calories: 117, Protein: 4 gm., Fat: 0 gm., Carbohydrates: 24 gm.

Tabbouleh
Bulgur* and Parsley Salad

This popular Middle Eastern salad has long been a staple for vegetarians, but it often contains ¾ cup or more of olive oil for a salad of this size. Our version contains no oil, but none of the flavor is missing! Mound the tabbouleh in a serving bowl or platter with a rim, and surround it with crisp, romaine lettuce leaves to use as scoopers. Decorate the top of the salad with tomato wedges, and sprigs of fresh mint and parsley (and a few Greek olives, for authenticity, if you like).

In a large serving bowl, mix together the bulgur and boiling water. Let stand while you prepare the vegetables and dressing.

To make the dressing, mix together the broth and cornstarch in a small saucepan. Stir over high heat until it boils. Continue stirring until thickened and clear, then remove from heat. Add the lemon juice, salt, and pepper, and whisk together well. Chill until time to add to the salad.

When the bulgur has absorbed all of the water, add the remaining salad ingredients and the dressing. Toss well and taste for salt and pepper. Refrigerate until serving time and present as instructed above.

*If you are allergic to wheat, use Rizcous, made by Lundberg Family Farms, instead of the bulgur wheat, following the directions on the package for preparation.

Serves 8 to 12

Per serving: Calories: 75, Protein: 3 gm., Fat: 0 gm., Carbohydrates: 15 gm.

---

1 c. dry bulgur wheat
1 c. boiling water

Dressing
¾ c. vegetarian broth
1½ tsp. cornstarch
¼ c. lemon juice
1 tsp. salt
black pepper to taste

4 c. fresh parsley, minced
2 ripe, firm tomatoes, diced
½ large cucumber, peeled and diced
½ large green bell pepper, seeded and chopped (optional)
½ c. fresh mint, chopped
½ c. green onion, chopped
1 T. dried dillweed (or 3 T. fresh, chopped)

Garnish
crisp romaine lettuce leaves
2 firm, ripe tomatoes, cut into wedges
fresh parsley and mint sprigs

Persian Orange Drink

T his refreshing beverage is sure to become a summer favorite.

4 c. freshly-squeezed orange juice
4 c. orange or tangerine-flavored
    sparkling mineral water
ice cubes
8 fresh mint sprigs
orange-blossom water (available from
    health food stores, Middle Eastern
    grocers, or pharmacies)

Mix together the orange juice and mineral water. Pour into 8 tall glasses with ice cubes. Sprinkle a few drops of orange-blossom water into each glass, and decorate each with a sprig of mint.

Serves 8

Per serving: Calories: 56, Protein: 1 gm., Fat: 0 gm., Carbohydrates: 3 gm.

Orange and Lemon Semolina Pudding

I t may seem unusual to use semolina cereal in a pudding, but this type of pudding is very common in the Middle East, and it is absolutely delicious, as well as very nutritious.

1½ c. water
3 c. orange juice
1½ c. sugar,
    or ¾ c. honey,
    or alternate sweetener
1 c. + 2 T. semolina cereal

¾ c. lemon juice
¾ T. lemon extract

Garnish
1½ tsp. ground cinnamon
4 tangerines, sectioned

Bring the water to a boil in a medium-sized pot. Add the orange juice, sugar, and semolina, and bring to a boil again, stirring. After it comes to a boil, pour the mixture into a mixing bowl, and add the lemon juice and extract. Beat the pudding with a hand-held electric beater for about 5 minutes, or until cool. Divide it between 8 pudding dishes, and sprinkle the tops with cinnamon. Decorate with the tangerine sections, cover with plastic wrap, and refrigerate until serving time.

Serves 8

Per serving: Calories: 276, Protein: 3 gm., Fat: 0 gm., Carbohydrates: 66 gm.

◇◇◇◇◇◇◇◇◇◇◇◇◇◇◇◇◇◇◇◇◇◇◇◇

Arabic Eid-Ul-Fitr Feast

Muslims all over the world celebrate Eid-Ul-Fitr, "the little festival" or Festival of the Fast-Breaking, which marks the end of Ramadan. (Ramadan is the month put aside by Muslims every year for prayer and fasting.) At the signal that Ramadan has ended (and in Islamic countries this can be with drums pounding and cannons booming!), there is joyous praising of Allah. But before anyone can begin feasting, they must give to the poor. Then, after prayers and special sermons, the feasting begins. The festivities can last for as long as three days, with many customs very similar to our Christmas or New Year celebrations: new clothes; gifts for the children from parents; special foods and lots of sweet treats; visits and meals with family and friends; music and street entertainment.

You could try a menu from any Islamic country, but here we present an Arabic-style feast (Arabic cooking encompasses the cuisines of the Arabian Peninsula, Lebanon, Syria, Jordan, and Egypt). If the weather permits, this meal is suitable to be made ahead and brought on a picnic, as many Muslim families do at this time. Most of the foods can be eaten at room temperature, and the Kusherie casserole can be brought in an insulated chest or wrapped in a blanket to keep warm.

This would also be a great spring equinox picnic party.

EID-UL-FITR
(End of Muslim Ramadan)
First Day of the 10th Month–New Moon

MENU

Fattoush
(pita bread and tomato salad with herbs)

Arabic "Pizzas"

Tamia
(bean patties)

Kusherie Casserole
(Egyptian rice, macaroni and lentils
with spicy tomato sauce and browned onions)

Arabic or pita bread

Sweet "Cheese" and Phyllo Turnovers

Fruit with Rosewater Syrup

juice or mint tea

Fattoush

Pita Bread and Tomato Salad with Herbs*

The seasonings of this salad will remind you of Tabbouleh (p. 53), however it is distinctly different and uniquely delicious! While it was originally invented, no doubt, as a way to use up stale pita bread, you can toast fresh bread for the same effect (similar to making croutons).

In Lebanon, you might find the herbs purslane and sumac in this salad, as well as pungent greens that are unfamiliar to us. In Lebanese restaurants here, fattoush is usually made simply with mint, parsley, and perhaps watercress—and it's always scrumptious! However, if you can find them, add the optional ground sumac (look for it in Middle Eastern grocery stores), arugula (a peppery, green, leafy vegetable also known as rocket), and purslane for a more authentic taste (you may have to grow the last two yourself—they are easy to grow).

Dressing
½ c. water or light vegetarian broth
1 tsp. cornstarch
⅓ c. lemon juice
1-2 cloves garlic, crushed
salt and freshly ground black pepper to taste
2 tsp. ground sumac (optional)

1 head of crisp romaine lettuce, washed, dried and torn up
1 medium cucumber, peeled and diced
2 large firm, ripe tomatoes, diced
4 green onions, chopped
½ c. fresh parsley, chopped (Italian or flat-leaf, if possible)
¼ c. fresh mint, chopped
1 green bell pepper, seeded and chopped (optional)
1 c. purslane, chopped (optional)
½-1 c. arugula or watercress leaves, torn, or a mixture (optional)

1 large pita bread, split, toasted, and broken into bite-size pieces

---

To make the dressing, mix the water or broth and cornstarch in a small saucepan, and stir over high heat until thickened and clear. Remove from heat and add the remaining dressing ingredients. Refrigerate to cool.

Just before serving the salad, place the lettuce in a large bowl. Add the remaining vegetables and herbs, and the broken-up, toasted pita bread. Add the dressing and toss well. Serve immediately.

*If you are allergic to wheat, use a toasted flatbread made from any grain you can tolerate, instead of the pita.

Serves 6

Per serving: Calories: 80, Protein: 3 gm., Fat: 0 gm., Carbohydrates: 15 gm.

Arabic "Pizzas"

These are often called Arabic, Lebanese, or Armenian "meat pies," because they are basically pita bread dough baked with a topping of minced meat, tomatoes, and herbs. Here, the topping is made with savory Vegetarian "Burger" instead of the meat and is baked on top of purchased (or your own homemade), soft pita breads for ease and convenience–and they are delicious! These make a great light lunch too.

Preheat the oven to 400°F.

To make the filling, mix the filling ingredients in the skillet in which the onions were steam-fried. Stir and cook briefly to heat and mix well. Spread the filling evenly over the 6 pita breads, and place them on ungreased cookie sheets. Bake for 10 minutes, or until the bottoms are slightly crisp. Serve hot or at room temperature with Tofu "Yogurt" to spread on top.

These can also be eaten with grilled eggplant on top for a quick meal.

Serves 6

Per serving: Calories: 215, Protein: 16 gm., Fat: 2 gm., Carbohydrates: 32 gm.

Filling
½ recipe for Vegetarian "Burger," cooked and crumbled (p. 171)
1 small onion, minced and steam-fried (use the juice from the canned tomatoes as the liquid for steam-frying)
½ c. canned tomatoes, drained and chopped
¼ c. parsley, chopped
1 tsp. lemon juice
½ tsp. ground cumin
¼ tsp. salt
liquid red pepper sauce and black pepper to taste

6 fresh, soft pita breads

Tofu "Yogurt" (p. 174) to serve with the "pizzas"

Tamia

Bean Patties

Tamia are the Arabic version of falafel, the Lebanese or Israeli chickpea balls that are so popular in North America now. (In fact, to make falafel, just substitute cooked or canned chickpeas for the lima beans in this recipe.) Tamia are usually made with fava beans, but large lima beans are substituted here, since they are similar and more readily available.

Instead of deep-frying the patties, we cook them in the oven; then, if you wish, brown them in just a tiny bit of olive oil. Instead of tahini sauce, serve them with liquid hot red pepper sauce and a low-fat Tofu-Mint or Parsley Sauce.

½ large onion
½ c. freshly parsley, chopped
3 cloves garlic
1½ c. cooked large dried lima beans, drained
2 slices French-type bread, crumbled and soaked in cold water to cover
1 T. lemon juice
1 tsp. ground cumin
½ tsp. EACH salt, dry basil, thyme, ground coriander and liquid hot pepper sauce
freshly ground black pepper to taste
whole wheat flour for dusting

Red Pepper Sauce (p. 59), or liquid hot pepper sauce for garnish
Tofu-Mint or Parsley Sauce (p. 59)

*1 T. extra-virgin olive oil

To make with a food processor, mince the onion, parsley, and garlic in the processor as finely as possible. Add the drained lima beans, and pulse until chopped. Squeeze the water out of the bread, and add to the processor along with the lemon juice, salt, spices, and hot pepper sauce. Process until well mixed. If the dough does not move freely, add 1 tablespoon water.

To make by hand, grate the onion, crush the garlic, and mince the parsley very fine. Mash the lima beans as smoothly as possible with a fork or a potato masher, or run through a food mill. Mix all of the ingredients together well with your hands (or run through a food grinder again) until well mixed and smooth.

Preheat the oven to 375°F. Form the dough into 16 equal-sized balls. Pat each ball into a ½-inch thick patty with neat edges, and dredge both sides in the flour. Place the patties on a lightly oiled cookie sheet. Bake for 10 minutes, then turn over and bake for another 10 minutes.

Serve the patties, with or without pita pockets, with the hot red pepper sauce and Tofu-

Mint or Parsley sauce (at right). If you serve them in pitas, add some lettuce, sliced onions, cucumber, and tomato.

Makes 16 patties

Per patty: Calories: 44, Protein: 3 gm., Fat: 1 gm., Carbohydrates: 7 gm.

Higher-Fat Option: To give the patties a slightly "crispy" crust and olive oil taste (but still with relatively little fat), just before serving, heat two heavy, 10-inch skillets, and add ¾ tsp. of olive oil to each pan. Place 8 patties in each pan, and fry them over medium-high heat until golden-brown on the bottom. Turn the patties over and add another ¾ tsp. olive oil to each pan, swirling it around so that each patty has some oil beneath it. Fry until golden brown.

Per patty: Calories: 51, Protein: 4 gm., Fat: 2 gm., Carbohydrates: 8 gm.

Tofu-Mint or Parsley Sauce

Blend together in a blender or food processor until very smooth: ½ *(10.5 oz.) pkg. reduced-fat, firm, SILKEN tofu, ¼ cup lemon juice, 2 cloves garlic, 1 tsp. dried mint (or 1 T. fresh), or ¼ cup fresh parsley, minced, ¼ tsp. salt, a pinch of sugar, and pepper to taste.*

Red Pepper Sauce

If you wish, you can make up this fresh hot peppper sauce instead of using a commercial variety. Mix in a sauce pan until simmering: *1 cup broth, 6 T. tomato paste, 2 tsp. harissa or Vietnamese red chili paste, 1 T. lemon juice, ½ tsp. ground cumin, 1 T. EACH minced parsley and cilantro (½ T. each dried).*

Kusherie Casserole

This very common Egyptian dish of rice, lentils, and macaroni with spicy tomato sauce and browned onions has been a family favorite for many years. The rice, lentils, and macaroni are usually served separately with the sauce alongside, but I find that this dish translates very well into a casserole, and it's easier to serve to a crowd or transport in this form.

Spicy Tomato Sauce
3½ c. tomato juice (can be drained from canned tomatoes)
1 (6 oz.) can tomato paste
1 green bell pepper, seeded and chopped
3 T. celery leaves, chopped
3 cloves garlic, chopped
1 T. sugar, honey, or alternate sweetener
1½ T. ground cumin
1 tsp. salt
¼ tsp. cayenne pepper

Rice and Lentils
1½ c. dried brown lentils
4 c. water
1½ c. long-grain brown rice
4 vegetarian or soy broth cubes
black pepper to taste

2 c. dry whole wheat or regular macaroni, cooked in boiling salted water until just done and drained

Browned Onions
3 large onions, sliced
4 cloves garlic, minced

To make the sauce, combine all of the sauce ingredients in a medium saucepan, and bring to a boil over high heat. Reduce heat and simmer, uncovered, 20-30 minutes.

To cook the rice and lentils, lightly oil a heavy pot, and add the lentils. Stir over high heat until they start to change color, then add the water, brown rice, vegetable cubes, and pepper. Cover and bring to a boil. Reduce heat to low and simmer (or bake in a 350°F oven) for 60 minutes.

Mix the cooked, drained macaroni with ¼ cup of the sauce.

To make the browned onions, steam-fry the onions and garlic in a lightly oiled skillet until soft and browned (using the directions on page 11).

To assemble the casserole, preheat the oven to 350°F. Oil a shallow 9" x 13" baking pan, and layer half the rice and lentils, the macaroni, the remaining rice and lentils, the sauce, and the browned onions, in that order. Cover with heavy foil and bake for half an hour. Serve the casserole with Tofu "Yogurt" (page 174).

Serves 8

Per serving: Calories: 419, Protein: 16 gm., Fat: 1 gm., Carbohydrates: 83 gm.

Sweet "Cheese" and Phyllo Turnovers

These subtly sweet, but delicious, "cheese" pastries are usually made with a ricotta-like soft cheese and are deep-fried. They are every bit as scrumptious when a sweet tofu filling is substituted and encased in a crisply baked phyllo pastry.

The flavoring is orange-blossom water, a flower extract that is used extensively in Middle Eastern cooking. It can be purchased in Middle Eastern or East Indian grocery stores, and some health food stores and pharmacies.

To make the filling, mix together the squeezed tofu, soymilk, sugar, orange-blossom water, and salt in a medium bowl. Set aside.

To fill the pastries, stack the phyllo sheets together with the edges even. Cut with scissors into four 6" x 5" rectangles. Keep the rectangles well covered with plastic wrap while you work.

Preheat the oven to 400°F. For each triangle, place a heaping tablespoon of filling in the lower left-hand corner of one phyllo rectangle (have the 5" sides at the bottom and top). Fold the right half of the rectangle over the left half, covering the filling. Now roll the filled end up, and keep folding over in this "flag" fashion, maintaining the triangle shape, until you come to the other end. (cont.)

8 oz. reduced-fat, firm tofu, crumbled and squeezed in a clean tea towel
¼ c. reduced-fat soymilk
2 T. sugar or alternate sweetener to taste
1 tsp. orange-blossom water
¼ tsp. salt

4 whole sheets of phyllo pastry, thawed and kept covered
soymilk or thawed frozen apple juice concentrate for brushing tops

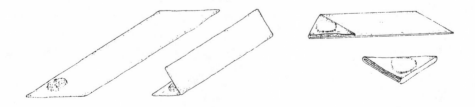

Place the filled triangles on lightly oiled baking sheets, not touching. Brush the tops with soymilk or apple juice concentrate, and bake for 15-20 minutes, or until golden and crispy. Place on wire cookie racks to cool. If they get soft on cooling, you can crisp them up in the oven again briefly.

Makes 16 turnovers

Per turnover: Calories: 36, Protein: 2 gm., Fat: 1 gm., Carbohydrates: 5 gm.

Fruit in Rosewater Syrup

R osewater is frequently used as a flavoring in Middle Eastern cooking, and it goes particularly well with fruit for a light dessert. Rosewater can be purchased in Middle Eastern or East Indian grocery stores, and some health food stores or pharmacies.

Rosewater Syrup (makes 3 c.)
1 c. mild honey
2 c. water
juice of ½ lemon
½ tsp. rosewater

fresh fruit of choice (about 1 c. per person), seeded, peeled, trimmed, and cut into bite-sized pieces

---

Place the water and honey in a medium saucepan, and bring to a boil over high heat. Reduce heat to low and simmer for 15 minutes. Add the lemon juice and rosewater, and cool.

To serve with fruit, pour the syrup over the prepared fruit, and refrigerate until ready to serve. Garnish with fresh mint, lemon balm, or rose petals.

Serves 8

Per serving: Calories: 229, Protein: 1 gm., Fat: 0 gm., Carbohydrates: 56 gm.

Cross-Cultural Seder Dinner

Passover is the Jewish festival of freedom, held every spring to commemorate the exodus of the Jews from slavery in Egypt, about 3,200 years ago. For the eight days of Passover, observant Jews eat no hametz—leavened bread, leavening agents, products made from flour, wheat, rye, barley, oats, and spelt.

Sephardic Jews* can eat all vegetables and many eat rice, but many observant Ashkenazic Jews* do not eat any grains, corn, string beans, peas, or dried legumes and beans. Ashkenazic Jews generally use potatoes (and potato starch or flour) and matzah, the unleavened Passover bread, which is like a large, thin cracker and can be made into crumbs or flour for Passover cooking and baking. The use of matzah commemorates the unleavened bread which was made for the journey out of Egypt. Such haste had to made when departing that there was no time to rise the bread.

Preparations for Passover in a kosher** home begin weeks before the holiday with scrupulous housecleaning (and removal of all hametz). All kitchen utensils and dishes for Passover are "koshered" by baking or boiling for the required times (families who can afford to do so have special Passover dishes and utensils used only at that time). New clothes are pur-

---

*"Sephardic" refers to Ladino-speaking Jews of the Iberian Peninsula and the Levant; "Ashkenazic" refers to Western and Central European, Yiddish-speaking Jews.

**"Kosher" means "according to the laws of Kashrut," the Jewish dietary laws which govern the selection, preparation, and consumption of all food for observant Jews.

PESACH OR PASSOVER
(Jewish Freedom Festival)
8 days beginning Nisan 15
(night of the Full Moon in late March
or early April)

CROSS-CULTURAL SEDER DINNER

*Yemenite Charoses
(Haroset)*

Eggplant Salad
with matzah

steamed fresh asparagus

Roasted Baby Potatoes with Rosemary

*Artichoke Stew
with Carrots and Mushrooms*

*Arugula and Beet Salad with Balsamic
Dressing*

dry white wine

*Almond-Scented Peach Crisp
with Matzah Crumb Topping*

chased for the children, if possible. At this time, one is also required to do some spiritual "housecleaning," as well.

A special dinner called a *seder* is held on the first and second nights of Passover, and special ceremonies on the last two nights end the festival. Friends and relatives dine together, and all participate in the reading of the Haggadah (which literally means "a recital"), the story of the Exodus, often with other readings which are relevant to current Jewish issues and struggles.

Besides the festive dinner, there are eight symbolic foods that are eaten at the seder:

✿ the matzah

✿ salt water, representing the tears of the Jews during their slavery in Egypt and other struggles

✿ green vegetables (karpas) such as parsley or celery to dip into the salt water, tokens of spring

✿ hard-boiled eggs to dip into the salt water as symbols of life and fertility (vegans can substitute boiled, oval potatoes, which are not Talmudically correct, but are traditional among Jewish vegans, according to Debra Wasserman of the Vegetarian Resource Group in Baltimore, Md.)

✿ horseradish or endive, or other "bitter herbs," symbolic of the bitterness of slavery

✿ haroset or charoses, a special mixture of fruit and nuts or seeds that is eaten between two pieces of matzah, symbolizing the mortar between the bricks of the structures the Hebrews were forced to build for the Egyptians

✿ a charred lamb shank bone to recall the ancient sacrifice in the temple (according to

Debra Wasserman, the Talmud allows a roasted beet, charred against a flame, to be substituted for the bone, because of its "fleshy" texture)

✿ wine, which is poured out at five times during the seder, symbolizing the sweetness of life and the fruits of the vine

After ceremonially partaking of the matzah and other symbolic foods during the reading of the Haggadah, the feasting begins!

Making Passover cooking and baking vegan is a challenge, to say the least. Beaten egg whites are commonly used as leavening during Passover, but it's not possible to use powdered egg replacer instead, because it contains a small amount of leavening. Since gluten and seitan, textured vegetable protein, tofu, soymilk, grains and beans, and grain syrups would also not be used by observant Jews, the possibilities are severely limited! However, commercial, low-fat almond "milk" or, for some people, commercial rice milks, might be used as a milk substitute; and for those who don't use sugar and honey, fruit syrups can be used. Potato starch, arrowroot, tapioca starch, and for some, rice flour can be used to thicken mixtures.

This menu could also be used for a spring equinox party.

Yemenite Charoses

Charoses, or haroset, is a mixture of fruit (sometimes dried, sometimes fresh, or a mixture), wine, spices, and nuts or seeds made into a sort of paste or "mortar." Most are too full of nuts for our purposes, but this spicy, Yemenite mixture contains only a small amount of Sesame Meal.

Combine the fruit, Sesame Meal, and ginger. Add red wine to moisten and matzah meal to make it cohesive, making it the consistency you prefer (like a thick spread).

Serves 10

Per serving: Calories: 150, Protein: 1 gm., Fat: 0 gm., Carbohydrates: 34 gm.

20 pitted dates, minced
20 dried figs, minced
2 T. Sesame Meal (p. 175)
2 tsp. ground ginger
pinch cayenne pepper (optional)
red wine
matzah meal

Eggplant Salad

There are many Middle Eastern versions of eggplant salad (actually, this is almost like a spread). Many of them contain far too much tahini for my taste. This garlicky version never fails to please.

Place the eggplant slices on lightly oiled cookie sheets; broil on both sides about 4" under the broiler element of your oven, until the slices are soft and slightly charred. (You can also grill these, if you prefer.)

Meanwhile, in a small, lightly oiled skillet, slowly steam-fry the garlic until it is soft, but not browned. In a medium bowl, coarsely mash the eggplant with a fork, and add the steam-fried garlic and other ingredients, mixing well.

Pack the salad into a serving bowl, and garnish with fresh parsley or cilantro. Serve cold or at room temperature.

Serves 8 to 10 as an appetizer

4 large eggplants, peeled and sliced ½" thick
16 cloves of garlic, peeled and chopped
¼ c. lemon juice
¼ c. red wine vinegar
¼ c. tomato puree (or 2 T. tomato paste mixed with 2 T. hot water)
2 tsp. ground cumin
2 tsp. paprika
1-2 tsp. salt
1 tsp. ground coriander
fresh parsley or cilantro for a garnish

Per serving: Calories: 77, Protein: 1 gm., Fat: 0 gm., Carbohydrates: 18 gm.

Roasted Baby Potatoes
with Rosemary

This is one of my all-time favorite recipes—in fact, I grow three rosemary plants to keep us in rosemary potatoes!

However, don't let lack of fresh rosemary keep you from making this treat—it's the best, but good-quality, dried rosemary also works well. I like it best with tiny, baby potatoes when they are in season, but it can be made with almost any type of potato, cut into small chunks.

These are usually made with copious amounts of olive oil, but my lemony Roasting or Grilling Marinade used instead results in crispy potatoes without a drop of oil.

This may seem like a lot of potatoes, but, in my experience, you can never have enough of these!

6 lbs. well-scrubbed potatoes, either whole, tiny ones or larger ones (about 16 medium potatoes), cut into large dice
1 recipe Roasting or Grilling Marinade, made with potato starch instead of cornstarch (p. 178)
⅓ c. fresh rosemary, chopped, or 2½-3 T. dried rosemary
salt to taste

Preheat the oven to 400°F.

In a large bowl, coat the potatoes with about 2½ cups of the marinade, and sprinkle with the rosemary and the salt to taste. Spread the potatoes on 4 large, lightly oiled, dark-colored cookie sheets.

Bake on both racks of a 30" oven, if you have one, switching the pans from top to bottom halfway through. (If you only have a small oven, bake two pans at a time, then combine them all into two pans, and warm them in the oven before serving.) Bake for about 1 hour, turning them several times with a spatula, until they are golden brown and crispy. Add the last bit of marinade if the potatoes are getting dry. Serve hot.

Serves 8 to 10

Per serving: Calories: 274, Protein: 3 gm., Fat: 0 gm., Carbohydrates: 64 gm.

Artichoke Stew
with Mushrooms and Carrots

This Greek-style vegetable stew, redolent of white wine, lemon, and dill, can be made ahead of time and reheated.

In a large, lightly oiled, heavy pot, steam-fry the onions, garlic, carrots, and mushrooms until the onions soften and the vegetables are beginning to brown a little. Add the artichokes, broth, wine, and dillweed, and bring to a boil. Then cover, turn the heat down, and simmer for 30 minutes. Add the parsley, lemon juice, and salt and pepper to taste (salt depends on the type of broth you use). Stir in the dissolved potato starch, and stir briefly until it has thickened. If it's still not thick enough for your taste, add another tablespoon of potato starch, dissolved. Serve hot.

For an everyday dish, omit the mushrooms and substitute 2 lbs. of small potatoes (or chunks). You may not need as much thickening for this. Eat as a one-dish meal with crusty bread.

Serves 8 to 10

Per serving: Calories: 104, Protein: 2 gm., Fat: 0 gm., Carbohydrates: 16 gm.

2 c. onions, chopped
6 cloves garlic, chopped
8 large carrots, peeled and cut into 1" chunks
1 lb. whole small mushrooms

2 (9 oz.) pkgs. frozen artichoke hearts, or 2 (14 oz.) cans artichoke hearts in water, drained
3 c. vegetarian or soy broth
1 c. dry white wine
1 T. dried dillweed

½ c. fresh parsley, chopped
juice of 1 lemon
salt and freshly ground black pepper to taste
1 T. potato starch dissolved in ¼ c. water

Arugula and Beet Salad
with Balsamic Dressing

A rugula (also known as rocket) is a dark, peppery green which has finally gained the popularity it deserves. It's still expensive to buy, but it grows easily, especially in spring and fall. If you have any tiny patch of ground, I recommend that you grow some (it grows like a weed, so you don't have to have a green thumb!).

Balsamic Dressing
1 c. water or light vegetarian broth
2 tsp. potato starch

½ c. balsamic vinegar
1-3 cloves of garlic, crushed
1½ tsp. salt,
   or 2 tsp. herbal salt

Salad
10 c. arugula leaves, cleaned and
   trimmed
2½ c. cooked or canned beets,
   julienned

Serves 8 to 10

Per serving: Calories: 15, Protein: 0 gm., Fat: 0 gm., Carbohydrates: 3 gm.

To make the dressing, place the water or broth and potato starch in a small saucepan, and stir constantly over high heat until the mixture thickens (it won't have to boil as it does with cornstarch). Whisk in the remaining dressing ingredients, then chill until serving time (at least 2 hours).

Just before serving, arrange the arugula leaves evenly on salad plates, then scatter the beets evenly over them. Drizzle each serving with some of the dressing.

You may vary the Balsamic Dressing as follows:

 - For a Dijon-Balsamic Vinaigrette, omit half of the salt, and add 1 ½ T. *dijon mustard*; a chopped green onion is optional.

 - You may add *2 T. brown sugar* if you like.

 - For Roasted Garlic Balsamic Vinaigrette, omit the raw garlic and use instead *10-12 cloves of garlic* which have been roasted in a foil packet at 350°F for 40 minutes. Use only ⅓ cup balsamic vinegar and 1 tsp. salt; add ¼ *tsp. pepper* and *1 T. Dijon mustard*, and blend everything in a blender or food processor until it's smooth and creamy. This is delicious!

Almond-Scented Peach Crisp
with Matzah Crumb Topping

This delectable dessert fits nicely into the cross-cultural theme of this seder dinner, a crisp being North American, the almond-flavored fruit having Middle Eastern undertones, and the matzah crumb topping being distinctly Jewish.

Preheat the oven to 350°F. In a 2-quart baking dish, combine the peaches, brown sugar, potato starch, and almond extract.

To make the topping, mix together the crumbs, honey, and cinnamon in a bowl until well combined. Sprinkle over the peaches. Bake for 25-35 minutes, or until bubbly with a golden brown top. Serve warm or at room temperature. If you like, pass some appropriate, non-dairy beverage (like commercial rice or almond "milk," vanilla or almond-flavored) to pour over each serving.

Serves 8 to 10

Per serving: Calories: 99, Protein: 1 gm., Fat: 0 gm., Carbohydrates: 23 gm.

8 c. sliced peaches (frozen and thawed is fine)
⅓ c. brown or turbinado sugar, or ¼ c. honey
1 T. potato starch
½ tsp. pure almond extract

Topping
1¼ c. matzah crumbs
¼ c. light honey or alternate liquid sweetener
1 tsp. ground cinnamon

EASTER
(Celebration of the Resurrection of Christ)
Sunday after the first Full Moon
after spring equinox

MENU

Antipasto

*Herbed Foccacia (p. 151)
and/or Crusty Bread (p. 149-50)*

Lasagne from the Garden

Frittata di Asparagi

Baby Peas, Florentine-style

*dry white wine
or Italian mineral water*

Rolled Strawberry "Ricotta" Cake

espresso

Italian Springtime Dinner

Spring holidays have been important to mankind since the dawn of time. They mark the end of winter and darkness, and the time when the earth comes back to life. Just as Christmas and other winter holidays are festivals of the return of light in the worldly and spiritual sense, Easter, Passover, and other spring holidays celebrate new life, new beginnings, and rebirth in both the physical and spiritual realms.

The word "Easter" stems from the name of the Saxon deity Eostre, Goddess of Spring. In most other Christian countries, however, the word for Easter is related to Passover—Pascua in Spanish, Pasqua in Italian, Pasen in Dutch, and Pask in Swedish, as just a few examples. In fact, until 325 C.E., early Christians observed Easter at the same time as the Jewish Passover, as the Last Supper was a Passover seder.

As with Christmas, many of our symbols of Easter come from pre-Christian sources. The rabbit represented birth and new life in ancient Egypt and was sacred to the goddess Eostre. In fact, her "Moon-hare" would lay eggs for good children—hence, the Easter bunny!

Since my paternal grandmother was Italian and Easter is such an important Italian holiday, I favor an Italian-style Easter dinner menu, fresh with spring vegetables, herbs, and fruit. You can serve it in the Italian style: antipasto with foccacia, bread, or breadsticks first; then the lasagne; then the fritatta and peas, with bread and wine throughout the meal. The dessert is for a special occasion, as Italians generally eat sweets as snacks.

Easter festivities in Italy, where the recipes for our Easter menu originate, are as rich and varied as the food. Easter breads, different ones in each region of Italy, abound. Check the recipe on page 148 for making your own Italian Easter bread.

Antipasto

" **A** ntipasto" literally means "before the pasta," or the appetizer. It can be very simple or very elaborate–I leave it up to you. (I've suggested commercial preparations whenever possible, for ease and convenience, since there are some very good ones on the market.) This is not really a recipe, but a guideline for composing your antipasto platter. Use the most attractive platter you can find, and arrange the foods artistically. Serve crusty bread, breadsticks, or the foccacia with the antipasto, but don't serve so much that everyone gets full!

Suggestions for the Antipasto Platter:
(use three or more)
commercial roasted peppers
Wine-Marinated Dried Tomatoes (p. 181)
Herbed Tofu "Feta" (p. 175)
raw vegetables, such as green onions
    and radishes
commercial marinated artichoke hearts
    (rinse off the oil), commercial
    caponata (Italian eggplant relish), and/
    or Italian pickled vegetables
commercial marinated mushrooms
grilled eggplant or zucchini
bean salad with herbs and a simple
    vinaigrette (p. 181)
commercial vegetarian "cold cuts"
commercial or homemade Vegetarian
    Antipasto Relish (p. 180)

Lasagne
From the Garden

This delicious lasagne is bound to become a favorite for company dinners. Your guests will find it difficult to believe that it was made not only without meat, but without cheese!

ALLERGY NOTE: If you have a wheat allergy, use about ¾ of a pound of brown rice fettucini or lasagne noodles instead of the wheat noodles.

15 whole wheat, spinach, or regular
   lasagne noodles, cooked, rinsed, and
   drained

Sauce
1 large onion, minced
4 cloves garlic, minced
1 large carrot, scrubbed and minced
1 medium zucchini, grated,
   or ½ large eggplant, minced
½ lb. mushrooms, sliced
1 (28 oz.) can diced tomatoes and juice
1 (6 oz.) can tomato paste
½ c. dried red wine (or water with 1 T.
   balsamic vinegar)
2 tsp. dried basil (or 2 T. fresh, chopped)
1 tsp. dried oregano (or 1 T. fresh,
   chopped)
1 tsp. salt
1 tsp. sugar or alternate sweetener
freshly ground black pepper to taste

Filling
3 (10.5 oz.) pkgs. reduced-fat, extra-firm,
   SILKEN tofu, well-mashed
1 (10 oz.) pkg. chopped spinach, thawed
   and squeezed dry,
   or 1 c. fresh parsley, minced
½ c. reduced-fat soymilk
1 tsp. salt
pinch of ground nutmeg

To make the sauce, mince the vegetables in a food processor if you have one, or by hand. In a large, heavy kettle, steam-fry the onion, garlic, carrot, zucchini, and mushrooms until they are getting soft. Add the tomatoes, tomato paste, wine, herbs, salt, sugar, and pepper. Bring to a boil, then turn down and let simmer, uncovered, while you make the filling and topping.

To make the filling, mix everything together thoroughly, and set aside.

To make the Tangy Cream Sauce, place the water, potato, onion, and salt (but not miso, if using) in a small pot, and bring to a boil. Cover and lower heat to a good simmer. Cook until the potato is tender. Place this (along with all the liquid and the miso, if using) in a blender or food processor with the remaining ingredients, and blend until very smooth. Set aside.

To assemble the lasagne, preheat the oven to 350°F. In a 9" x 13" flat baking pan, spread evenly ¼ of the tomato sauce. Top with 5 of the noodles, then ½ the filling (and a sprinkling of soy parmesan, if you like), layering evenly. Spread on another ¼ of the tomato sauce; add 5 more noodles and the rest of the filling (and more soy parmesan, if you like). Top with another ¼ of the tomato sauce, then the remaining 5 noodles. Spread the remaining tomato sauce over the noodles (and a sprinkling of soy parmesan). Pour on the Tangy Cream Sauce to make a thin layer on top (you probably won't use it all). If you like, sprinkle the top with breadcrumbs. (You can put this together ahead of time and bake it later—if it's chilled, add about 15 minutes to the baking time.)

Bake for 40 minutes, then let the casserole stand for 10 minutes before serving. (If it's browning too much, cover it loosely with foil.)

Serves 8

Per serving: Calories: 368, Protein: 22 gm., Fat: 3 gm., Carbohydrates: 61 gm.

Tangy Cream Sauce
1½ c. water
1 medium potato, peeled and chunked
½ medium onion, peeled and chunked
1 tsp. salt,
    or 1 T. light miso plus ½ tsp. salt
4 oz. reduced-fat, firm or medium firm,
    regular tofu, crumbled
4 T. nutritional yeast flakes
1 T. Sesame Meal (p. 175)
1 T. lemon juice
pinch of garlic granules
soy parmesan (optional)
breadcrumbs

Baby Peas, Florentine-Style

I f you have access to very tiny, freshly-picked early peas, by all means use them in this dish. Otherwise, use frozen petite peas (tiny baby peas), not mature peas.

In place of the traditional prosciutto or pancetta ham, we use chopped "veggie back bacon" or soy bacon chips which are soaked in hot water to soften. Make this dish at the last minute.

In a large, heavy skillet, cook the peas with about ⅓ cup water over medium heat, covered, for 5 minutes (for frozen, about 10 minutes for fresh), or just until tender and still bright green. Drain off any remaining water. Stir in the parsley, "back bacon" or soy bacon chips, and the spread. Toss well with salt to taste and a few twists of the pepper mill. Serve immediately.

Serves 8

Per serving: Calories: 54, Protein: 4 gm., Fat: 0 gm., Carbohydrates: 9 gm.

---

2 (10 oz.) pkgs. frozen petite peas,
    thawed,
    or 4 lbs. (unshelled weight) early
    peas, shelled
¼ c. fresh parsley, minced
¼ c. "veggie back bacon," minced,
    or 2 T. soy bacon chips soaked in
    hot water to cover for 10 minutes,
    then drained
¼ c. Garlic Guilt-Free Bread-Spread
    (p. 177)
freshly ground black pepper

Frittata Di Asparagi
Eggless Italian "Omelet" with Asparagus

A frittata is an Italian omelet, similar to the Spanish "tortilla" (not the same as the tortilla bread of Mexico). It's a great luncheon or light supper dish and is really at its best when cool, so it's a good make-ahead dish. In this recipe, lightly seasoned, blended tofu provides an egg-free showcase for spring asparagus, a favorite Italian vegetable—but feel free to substitute other vegetables according to the season.

1 lb. reduced-fat, firm, regular tofu
1½ c. water or reduced-fat soymilk (or just enough so that the mixture will blend)
2 T. nutritional yeast flakes
1 T. soy sauce
1 tsp. salt
½ tsp. onion powder
¼ tsp. garlic granules

4 c. fresh asparagus, cut into 2" lengths and lightly-steamed
2 T. fresh parsley or basil, minced
soy parmesan (optional)

Preheat the oven to 350°F. Lightly oil two 9" or 10" cast iron skillets or pie pans. Blend the tofu, water or soymilk, yeast, soy sauce, salt, onion powder, and garlic granules in the blender until very smooth. Divide the asparagus between the two pans. Pour the blended mixture over the asparagus, dividing evenly. Smooth the tops and sprinkle with the fresh herbs.

Bake for 30 minutes. Loosen the edges and bottoms, and carefully invert onto lightly oiled cookie sheets. Bake 10 minutes more. If desired, sprinkle with soy parmesan.

Let come to room temperature before cutting into wedges and serving.

Serves 8 (two 9" or 10" frittatas)

Per serving: Calories: 87, Protein: 9 gm., Fat: 3 gm., Carbohydrates: 7 gm.

Rolled Strawberry "Ricotta" Cake

This almond-scented cake is light, like an Italian sponge cake. Instead of the usual ricotta cheese filling, we use a creamy strawberry and tofu mixture.

To make the cake roll, prepare the Basic Holiday Cake Roll, using two-thirds of the Strawberry "Ricotta" Filling shown on this page instead of the *Sweet "Cream Cheese" Filling.* (Pass the rest for a topping.)

To make the filling, mix the sugar, water, lemon juice, and agar powder in a small saucepan, and let soak for 5 minutes. Bring to a boil over high heat, stirring until the sugar is dissolved. Stir in the crumbled tofu and the strawberries, and mix over high heat until they are hot (this is important so that the agar doesn't gel too fast). Pour the mixture into a blender or food processor, and blend until quite smooth. Chill in a bowl until spreadable.

Continue to fill and roll as for the Holiday Cake Roll. Just before serving, carefully cut the roll into 8 even slices, garnish with fresh strawberries, and serve with the remaining Strawberry "Ricotta" Filling.

Serves 8

Per serving: Calories: 248, Protein: 8 gm., Fat: 1 gm., Carbohydrates: 52 gm.

Basic Holiday Cake Roll, almond
   variation (p. 154-55)

Strawberry "Ricotta" Filling
1 pkg. (10.5 oz.) reduced-fat, extra-firm,
   SILKEN tofu, crumbled
2 c. fresh strawberries, sliced (or
   unsweetened frozen, thawed)
½ c. sugar or alternate sweetener
¼ c. water
1 T. lemon juice
1 tsp. agar powder,
   or 2 T. agar flakes
fresh strawberries for garnish

WESAK OR VISAKHA PUJA

(Birth, Death, and Enlightenment of Buddha)
About the second Sunday in May,
on the full moon

MENU

Thai Corn "Fritters"

Thai Tofu Salad

Sweet and Sour Vegetables

jasmine rice

Crispy Wrapped Baked Bananas

low-fat, non-dairy, vanilla frozen dessert

Thai tea (iced or hot)
or lemonade

◆◇◆◇◆◇◆◇◆◇◆◇◆◇◆◇◆◇◆◇◆◇◆

Thai Visakha Puja Feast

Like Christians and Jews, Buddhists have long celebrated spring with merry festivities. In Sri Lanka, Buddhists celebrate the birth, death, and enlightenment of Buddha on the three days of Wesak. In Thailand, the same festival is known as Visakha Puja, and homes and temples are decorated with paper lanterns for special services.

There are more than 24 practicing Buddhist sects in North America today, and some celebrate Buddha's birthday as a separate festival—such as the Japanese Kambutsue on April 8th, when small, flower-covered shrines are built over the statues of the infant Buddha. The statues are bathed with sweet, scented tea by worshipers. In North America, many Buddhist groups join together to celebrate Wesak with prayers, meditation, a vegetarian feast, and multicultural singing and dancing.

The following delightful menu includes one of my favorite dishes, Thai Corn Fritters—however, instead of being deep-fried, they are baked (the addition of powdered gluten to the batter helps them puff up as if they were fried). The dessert is a fritter-like, baked banana dish, wrapped in crispy phyllo pastry instead of a deep-fried batter.

If you can find imported Thai tea leaves, by all means serve Thai tea—the tea leaves have been specially treated to give them a distinctive, vanilla-like flavor and deep orange color. Otherwise, serve a Thai-style iced tea made with ordinary tea leaves, sweet and milky, but served over ice. Lemonade, another favorite Thai drink, is also a good beverage choice.

A note about the jasmine rice suggested in this menu: this is a fragrant, long-grained rice that is widely available in North America. It can be steamed just as you would any long-grain rice. If you can't find it, substitute basmati or other long-grained rice.

This menu would make a good company meal any time of the year, for friends who enjoy spicy foods.

Thai Corn "Fritters"

These crispy treats are a cinch to make.

Make the Sweet Red Chile Sauce ahead of time. Combine the sauce ingredients in a small saucepan, and boil until reduced to ⅔ cup. Set aside.

Preheat the oven to 400°F.

Combine the gluten powder, breadcrumbs, broth powder, salt, onion powder, and pepper in a dry bowl. Add the corn, garlic, and cilantro, and mix well. *If you have a food processor*, mince the garlic and cilantro in it, add the corn, and process coarsely, then add the contents of the bowl, and pulse just to mix.

When the mixture is well-combined, form it into 1½" balls, and press them into little patties. Place on lightly oiled or non-stick cookie sheets, lightly cover with foil, and bake for 10 minutes. Turn them over, covering again lightly, and bake 10 minutes more. Serve hot with the Sweet Red Chile Sauce to dip the "fritters" into.

Serves 6

Per serving: Calories: 197, Protein: 9 gm., Fat: 0 gm., Carbohydrates: 40 gm.

Sweet Red Chile Sauce
¾ c. sugar, honey, or alternate sweetener
¾ c. cider or rice vinegar
1 dried red chile
½ tsp. salt

Batter
6 T. pure gluten powder (vital wheat gluten)
½ c. fine fresh breadcrumbs
2 tsp. chicken-style vegetarian broth powder
1 tsp. salt
½ tsp. onion powder
½ tsp. black pepper

12 oz. drained, canned or frozen corn (or 2½ c. fresh corn kernels), chopped or ground
4 cloves garlic, crushed
2 T. fresh cilantro, minced (or 1 T. dried)

1 T. garlic, minced
6 whole baby corn (canned is fine)
24 chunks of canned pineapple
½ cucumber, peeled and cut into rounds
3 medium onions, halved and thinly sliced
3 medium-ripe but firm tomatoes, quartered
6 green onions, cut into 1" pieces
2 large, red bell peppers, seeded and cut into thin strips

3 T. light soy sauce
1 T. sugar or alternate sweetener
1 tsp. white pepper
1 tsp. (or less, according to taste) dried red chile flakes
1 T. cornstarch mixed with ¾ c. cold water

Sweet and Sour Vegetables

*T*his easy Thai stir-fry can be thrown together *at the last minute if you have the vegetables prepared. It's hot!*

Lightly oil a large wok or skillet, and heat over high heat. Add the garlic and a few sprinkles of water; stir-fry for a few seconds, until the water evaporates. Add each vegetable or fruit listed in turn, stirring constantly and adding just a bit of water, if needed, to keep from sticking. When the vegetables are crisp-tender, add the soy sauce, sugar, white pepper, chile, then the cornstarch mixture; stir until it has thickened. Turn onto a serving dish, and serve immediately with steamed jasmine rice.

Serves 6

Per serving: Calories: 207, Protein: 2 gm., Fat: 0 gm., Carbohydrates: 49 gm.

6 oz. rice vermicelli (or thin, Thai rice noodles)
2 lbs. prepared Pan-Fried Breast of Tofu (p. 172), Smoky Pan-Fried Tofu (p. 172) , or any commercial, savory, marinated tofu (cooked), cut into slivers
1 cucumber, peeled and cut into thin strips about 2-3" long
1½ large red bell peppers, seeded and cut into thin strips
⅓ c. fresh mint, basil, or cilantro, chopped

Thai Tofu Salad

*T*his makes a great, hot-weather main dish all on *it's own. It's so easy to throw together and can be made ahead of time.*

In a large bowl, cover the rice vermicelli with boiling water. Let it stand for 3 minutes, or until softened, then drain and rinse well. Combine the vermicelli in the bowl with the tofu, cucumber, bell pepper, and fresh herbs.

(cont.)

Whisk the dressing ingredients together, and pour over the salad. Toss well. Serve at room temperature on a platter decorated with fresh mint, basil, and/or cilantro.

Serves 6

Per serving: Calories: 278, Protein: 17 gm., Fat: 2 gm., Carbohydrates: 49 gm.

Dressing
6 T. light soy sauce
4½ T. fresh lime juice
3 T. sugar or alternate sweetener
1½ T. fresh ginger, minced
1½ T. pickled jalapeño pepper, minced
1 large clove garlic, crushed

Crispy Wrapped Baked Bananas

These are very easy to make, and the contrast between the hot, crispy, baked bananas and the cold, creamy, non-dairy vanilla dessert is delicious! Serve immediately after baking.

If the phyllo sheets are frozen, thaw them; cut them in half vertically, and keep well covered. Peel the bananas and brush them with lemon juice to keep from discoloring.

Preheat the oven to 400°F.

To make each wrapped banana, place one banana at the bottom (short end) of half a phyllo sheet, and sprinkle the banana with 1 tsp. of Sucanat or brown sugar and ¼ tsp. coconut extract. Roll the dough over it once, then fold in the outer edges, and keep rolling away from you. Place the wrapped bananas on a lightly oiled cookie sheet, and brush the tops with apple juice. Bake for 15 to 20 minutes, or until golden and crispy. Serve immediately with a scoop of the frozen dessert on each plate.

3 whole sheets of phyllo pastry
6 medium ripe bananas
2 T. Sucanat or brown sugar
1½ tsp. coconut extract
apple juice for brushing

about 1½ pints non-dairy, vanilla frozen dessert of your choice (low-fat, commercial, or homemade) (p. 166-67)

Serves 6

Per serving: Calories: 240, Protein: 6 gm., Fat: 1 gm., Carbohydrates: 52 gm.

INDEPENDENCE DAY
CANADA DAY

July 4/July 1
(respectively)

MENU

Baked Tortilla Chips
commercial or homemade (p.179)
with
Homemade Tomato Salsa
and Low-fat Guacamole

Gazpacho
or sliced fresh tomatoes

Four-Bean Salad

Hard Rolls
commercial or homemade (p. 149-50)

Barbecued "Ribs"
with Smoky Chipotle Barbecue Sauce

Freeform Peach Pie

low-fat, non-dairy, vanilla frozen dessert
commercial or homemade (p. 166–67)

Picnic-Barbecue

What would our 4th/1st of July celebration meals be like in North America if these historic occasions had occurred in the dead of winter rather than mid-summer? No picnics, no barbecues—it doesn't bear thinking about!

In the United States, Independence Day is celebrated on the 4th of July. Canada celebrates her national birthday party on July 1st (formerly known as Dominion Day), the official date of the unity of the provinces as one country. In both countries, parades, outdoor concerts, dances, special citizenship ceremonies, and, of course, barbecues and picnics, are the order of the day.

Do barbecues mean meat to you? They don't have to—with the popularity of grilled everything-under-the-sun, you can marinate any of your favorite foods (tofu, eggplant, sweet potatoes, etc.) in barbecue sauce, and enjoy their slightly-charred, smoky goodness while the carnivores court heavy-duty heartburn (not to mention carcinogens!).

Another alternative is to bring along some commercial tofu hot dogs (these are best if boiled before barbecuing) or firm vegetarian burgers. (Check out page 185 for some books on vegetarian barbecuing.) Try our recipe for Barbecued "Ribs" with Smoky Chipotle Barbecue Sauce.

The following picnic/barbecue menu would also be good for a May Day celebration (if the weather is good) or a summer solstice, graduation, Father's Day, or birthday party.

Homemade Tomato Salsa

I n the northern U.S. and Canada, most of us don't get really ripe tomatoes in our gardens until at least August, and the fresh ones in the stores aren't always very tasty, so this is the salsa I make most of the year. Everyone agrees that it is so much better than the store-bought kind! (The cilantro is optional because my family doesn't like it.) Our neighbors in more southern states might find this recipe useful as a winter salsa too.

If you have a food processor, this is a snap to make.

If you have a food processor, pulse the garlic cloves, then add the onion, green pepper, and the jalapeños, and pulse until minced. Add the drained tomatoes and the remaining ingredients, and pulse until well mixed.

If you don't have a food processor, finely chop the onion, garlic, green pepper, and jalapeños with a sharp knife or a food mill. Mix in a bowl with the remaining ingredients. (If the tomatoes are too chunky for your taste, chop or grind them up too.)

Keep in tightly-closed jars in the refrigerator. It will keep refrigerated for several weeks (if it's not eaten first!). Some clear liquid will rise to the top—pour it off or stir it in, depending on the consistency you like.

Makes about 5 cups

Per ¼ cup: Calories: 22, Protein: 1 gm., Fat: 0 gm., Carbohydrates: 5 gm.

8 cloves garlic
1 large onion, cut in chunks
1 large green pepper, seeded and cut in chunks
¼ c. drained pickled jalapeño peppers, or 2 or 3 fresh seeded hot green chilies

2 (28 oz.) cans diced tomatoes, very well drained
¼ c. tomato paste
2 T. lemon juice
1-2 tsp. salt
1 tsp. dried oregano (or 1 T. fresh)
¼ c. fresh cilantro, chopped (optional)
1 tsp. dried red chile flakes (if you like it really hot–but remember that this salsa gets hotter the longer it sits around!)

Gazpacho

1 (48 oz.) can good-quality tomato juice
   or tomato-vegetable cocktail
1 medium onion, minced
1 green bell pepper, seeded and chopped
1 large ripe, firm tomato, chopped
½ large cucumber, peeled and diced
   small
¼ c. red wine vinegar or balsamic vinegar
2 T. fresh parsley or basil, minced
2 cloves garlic, crushed
1 tsp. sugar, honey, or alternate
   sweetener
1 tsp. Vegetarian Worcestershire Sauce
   (p. 176)
1 tsp. salt
Croutons (p. 178)

*I*f you think that gazpacho, the famous Spanish *"soup-salad," has to be swimming in olive oil, you're in for a treat! We keep this in the refrigerator all summer for quick snacks or a ready-made first course for company. (I like this better with hand-chopped vegetables.)*

Combine all the ingredients in a large bowl or pitcher. Stir well, cover, and chill until serving time. Serve with croutons.

Makes about 2 quarts

Per cup: Calories: 42, Protein: 1 gm., Fat: 0 gm., Carbohydrates: 8 gm.

Low-Fat Guacamole

*B*orn and raised in California, I love avocados, but their high fat content makes them a rare treat. The following easy bean mixture (a variation of the one in my first cookbook, The Almost No-Fat Cookbook) makes a very tasty alternative. You need a food processor for this recipe.*

10 oz. whole, small green beans (frozen
   are fine)
10 oz. frozen baby lima beans
1 c. medium-firm, reduced-fat, regular
   tofu,
   or 1 (10.5 oz.) pkg. firm or extra-firm,
   reduced-fat, SILKEN tofu
½ c. tomato salsa
4-6 T. lemon juice
4 cloves garlic, crushed
2 tsp. salt
1 tsp. ground cumin

Cook the beans (both kinds) separately in water just to cover for about 5 minutes, or just until completely tender but not mushy. Drain the beans and place in the food processor; process until smooth. Add the remaining ingredients and process again until smooth. Place in a covered bowl, and refrigerate.

Makes about 4 cups

Per ¼ cup: Calories: 43, Protein: 3 gm., Fat: 1 gm., Carbohydrates: 6 gm.

Four-Bean Salad for a Crowd

This delicious salad, oil-free and with much less sweetener than the traditional bean salad, is always a hit at potlucks.

To make the dressing, mix the broth or water and the cornstarch together in a medium saucepan, and stir constantly over high heat until the mixture turns thick and clear and boils for a few minutes. Remove from the heat and whisk in the remaining ingredients.

Mix the dressing together with the salad ingredients in a large bowl or rigid plastic container with a lid. Refrigerate for several hours or days, stirring or shaking before serving.

Makes about 1 gallon

Per cup: Calories: 260, Protein: 12 gm., Fat: 1 gm., Carbohydrates: 49 gm.

Sweet and Sour Italian Dressing
3 c. water or light vegetarian broth
2 T. cornstarch
2 c. red wine vinegar or cider vinegar
⅓ c. honey, sugar, or alternate
    sweetener
9 cloves garlic, crushed
2 T. salt
1 T. Vegetarian Worcestershire Sauce
    (p. 176)
1 T. freshly ground black pepper
1 T. dry mustard

5 c. cooked or canned chickpeas,
    drained (2 c. dry)
5 c. cooked or canned small red beans
    or kidney beans, drained (2 c. dry)
5 c. cooked or canned blackeyed peas,
    drained (2 c. dry)
5 c. cooked small, whole green beans
    (frozen are fine), snapped in half
8 large green onions, trimmed and
    chopped
2-3 c. celery, chopped
1 c. fresh parsley, chopped

Freeform Peach Pie, p. 85

Barbecued "Ribs"
with Smoky Chipotle Barbecue Sauce

The "ribs" are actually baked gluten balls, which are easily made in your oven from pure gluten powder and water. They bake up puffy and golden, but, when covered with barbecue sauce (you can use your own favorite—but this is one of the best!), and briefly baked again, they are gooey and chewy and hard to stop eating! These should be made ahead of time. They can then be reheated briefly on the barbecue, if you wish.

Chipotle chiles in adobado sauce can be purchased in cans from Latin American grocery stores or health food stores. Puree the contents of the can, and keep in a covered jar in the refrigerator. Chipotles are actually smoked, dried jalapeño peppers, so they are hot. They lend a delicious smoky flavor to sauces and vegetarian chilies.

Baked Gluten Balls
2½ c. pure gluten powder (vital wheat gluten)
2 c. COLD water

Smoky Chipotle Barbecue Sauce (makes 6 c.):
2 medium onions, minced
4 cloves garlic, minced
2 large (28 oz.) cans tomatoes and juice, blended in a blender or food processor until smooth (or use crushed tomatoes)
1 c. brown sugar or Sucanat, (or turbinado sugar with 2 T. molasses)
½ c. red wine vinegar
¼ c. Vegetarian Worcestershire Sauce (p. 176)
2 T. pureed chipotle chiles in adobado sauce
1 T. salt
2 tsp. mustard powder
2 tsp. liquid smoke

Per serving: Calories: 210, Protein: 27 gm., Fat: 1 gm., Carbohydrates: 24 gm.

To make the baked gluten balls, mix the gluten powder and water together in a medium bowl until it forms a smooth dough. Preheat the oven to 375°F. Cut the dough into about 8 dozen equal-sized pieces, and place them a couple of inches apart on lightly oiled cookie sheets. Bake for 15-20 minutes, or until quite puffy and golden.

(If you don't want to use all of them at once, you can freeze them in plastic bags. They can also be sliced and used in stir-fries or Chinese sweet and sour dishes.)

To make the barbecue sauce, steam-fry the onion and garlic in a large, heavy saucepan until they soften. Add the remaining ingredients, and simmer for 30 minutes. If you aren't using it right away, the sauce will keep in jars in the refrigerator for many weeks.

To cook the "ribs," preheat the oven to 350°F. Place the gluten puffs on lightly oiled cookie sheets, and pour the barbecue sauce over them (you will need about 4 cups). Bake for 15 minutes.

Serves 10 to 12

Freeform Peach Pie
with Berry Sauce

I f you thought you had to give up summer fruit pies when you embarked on a very-low-fat style of eating, think again! Using our tender, fat-free Yeasted Pastry, you can indulge in juicy, delectable pies during the whole harvest season! A freeform crust gives the dessert a pleasant, rustic appearance (see illustration, p. 83).

For a patriotic effect, Americans can serve the pie with a raspberry sauce (red—see the Raspberry Coulis on p. 33), low-fat, non-dairy, vanilla frozen dessert (white), and a scattering of fresh blueberries (blue); Canadians can omit the blueberries to mimic the red and white of the Maple Leaf flag with only the raspberry sauce and frozen dessert. This pie is naturally sweetened with frozen juice concentrate, but Canadians might like to add a northern touch by using maple syrup as the sweetener.

In a small saucepan, mix together the maple syrup or juice concentrate and the cornstarch. Stir constantly over medium-high heat until it is thick and clear. Stir in the lemon juice, salt, almond extract, nutmeg, and cinnamon. Pour over the peaches in a bowl. Set aside and preheat the oven to 350°F.

On a floured surface, roll the Yeasted Pastry Dough out into a 16" circle. (It doesn't have to be perfect, but don't leave any holes or very thin spots.) Carefully transfer the dough circle to a lightly oiled cookie sheet or pizza pan. Pile the peach filling in the middle of the circle, and bring up the edges around the filling to make a 10" freeform pie, pleating the edges of the dough over the filling and leaving about a 5" open circle in the middle (see illustration, p. 83).

Bake the pie for about 25 minutes, then brush the pie lightly with a little maple syrup or thawed juice concentrate, and bake 5 minutes more, or until golden brown. Serve hot or at room temperature.

Have ready
Yeasted Pastry Dough for one 10" freeform pie (p. 163)

Filling
5 c. fresh peaches, peeled and sliced
½ c. maple syrup or thawed frozen apple juice concentrate, plus a little more to brush on the crust*
2 T. cornstarch
1 tsp. lemon juice
¼ tsp. salt
¼ tsp. pure almond extract
¼ tsp. freshly ground nutmeg
¼ tsp. ground cinnamon

*In some areas you can get peach juice concentrate or a mixture of apple, peach, and pear juice concentrates— use one of these instead of apple juice concentrate if you like.

1 freeform pie (serves 8 to 12)

Per serving: Calories: 142, Protein: 2 gm., Fat: 0 gm., Carbohydrates: 33 gm.

ROSH HASHANAH

(Jewish New Year)

Tishri 1 and 2
(roughly corresponding with September,
on the New Moon)

MENU

Potato and Green Bean Salad

Vegetable Goulash
with Tofu Sour Cream (p. 174) and
Savory Noodle Kugel

Cabbage Strudel

Spiral Challah
with Raisins (p. 145)

Jewish Honey Cake (p. 153)
and/or Plum Kuchen

beer, juice, or dry red wine

◆◆◆◆◆◆◆◆◆◆◆◆◆◆◆◆◆◆◆◆◆◆◆

Late Summer Rosh Hashanah Meal

Rosh Hashanah literally means "the head of the year," but it's often called "the Birthday of the World." On Rosh Hashanah, Jews greet each other, wishing, "May you be inscribed in the Book of Life for a happy year!" This is also the traditional time of year to send greeting cards to friends and loved ones. In the synagogue, the shofar, or ram's horn, is blown to remind those who hear it to lead good lives. As a symbol of new beginnings and purity, the Torah mantles and Ark curtains in the synagogues are white, and worshipers often wear white as well.

Besides emphasizing the wonderful fruits of the summer harvest at this time of year, our menu recognizes the traditional accent on sweet foods (particularly honey), symbolizing hopes for a sweet year, and round foods, signifying hopes for a full and solid year. A special, spiral-shaped or round version of challah, the fluffy Sabbath bread, is often made, sometimes with raisins or currants added. Desserts abound, not surprisingly with the emphasis on sweets! Plum and apple desserts (made from round fruits) such as strudels, pies, and cakes, are popular, as is the traditional Jewish Honey Cake or Lekakh.

Traditionally, honey is kept on the table from Rosh Hashanah through Sukkot (Jewish Feast of the Ingathering). Challah is dipped in it and, on the first night of Rosh Hashanah, round apple slices are dipped into the honey and eaten. (On the second night it is customary to eat a new fruit, one that has not been eaten yet that season.) If you have nutritional, allergic, or ethical objections to honey, use a fruit concentrate syrup or a grain syrup instead.

This lovely harvest meal would be suitable also for a Shavuot or Purim dinner, a bar or bat mitzvah or Brit Milah party, or for a summer solstice or Lammas celebration.

Potato and Green Bean Salad

This is my version of a French salad made with fresh green beans and new boiling potatoes. Now I find I can enjoy it year-round, using waxy, red-skinned potatoes and the frozen, small, whole green beans that are so much better than cut, frozen green beans.

Cover the potatoes with water, and bring to a boil. Cover and simmer until they are tender, but still firm. Drain in a colander and peel them with your fingers under running cold water. Drain them again and cut into medium dice, or thick slices, as desired. Toss the potatoes in a serving bowl with the white wine, green onions, tarragon, and salt and pepper to taste. Set aside.

Cook the green beans in boiling water to cover for about 5 minutes, or until crisp-tender. Drain and cool under cold running water. Drain well again. Fold the green beans into the potatoes.

To make the vinaigrette, stir the cornstarch and broth together in a small saucepan. Stir constantly over high heat until the broth thickens and clears. Whisk in the vinegar and salt. Pour the hot mixture over the potatoes and beans, and stir gently, sprinkling with pepper to taste.

Refrigerate the salad until ready to serve. Toss the salad gently and taste for salt. Arrange the tomato wedges decoratively on top, and serve cold or at room temperature on crisp romaine lettuce leaves, if you like.

Serves 8 to 12

4 lbs. new boiling potatoes or red-skinned potatoes (cut into equal-sized chunks if too large to cook whole), unpeeled

¼ c. dry white wine or white wine vinegar
¼ c. green onion, minced
¼ c. fresh tarragon, minced (or 4 tsp. dried)
salt and freshly ground black pepper to taste

1 lb. fresh green beans, ends trimmed and cut into 2" pieces, or frozen, whole, small green beans, snapped in half

Vinaigrette
1 c. cold, light vegetarian broth
2 tsp. cornstarch
⅓ c. white wine vinegar
1-1½ tsp. salt
freshly ground black pepper

4 small ripe, firm tomatoes, cut into wedges

Per serving: Calories: 184, Protein: 3 gm., Fat: 0 gm., Carbohydrates: 42 gm.

Vegetable Goulash
Hungarian-Style Stew

This is a very elegant stew, made with dry red wine as the liquid (use a good, dry kosher wine, if you like), but so easy to put together—and then it just cooks itself in the oven! Serve the goulash over the Savory Noodle Kugel on the next page with Tofu Sour Cream on the side. (Or, for a less festive occasion, just serve it over plain, boiled fettucine pasta, broken in half, which has been moistened with Tofu Sour Cream and seasoned with salt and pepper.)

If you prefer a "meaty" stew, use the reconstituted textured vegetable protein chunks. For an all-vegetable stew, use eggplant chunks instead—either way, it's delicious!

1 large green bell pepper, seeded and
    cut into 1" squares
1 large onion, thickly sliced
4 cloves garlic, minced

1 medium eggplant, cubed,
    or 2 c. rehydrated textured vegetable
    protein chunks (1⅓ c. dry—p. 169)
1 large (28 oz.) can tomatoes with juice
2 bay leaves
8 medium waxy (boiling) potatoes,
    quartered
3 large carrots, peeled and chunked
12 medium mushrooms, halved
2 c. dry red wine
1 T. dried dillweed
1 T. paprika
1 T. mushroom soy sauce
about 1 T. salt
1 tsp. sugar or alternate sweetener
freshly ground black pepper to taste

¼ c. fresh parsley, minced (optional)
Tofu Sour Cream (p. 174), for topping

Preheat the oven to 350°F.

In a large, lightly oiled, heavy pot which can go into the oven (cast iron is fine), steam-fry the pepper, onion, and garlic until the onion starts to soften. Add the eggplant or textured vegetable protein, the tomatoes (breaking them up a bit), bay leaves, potatoes, carrots, mushrooms, wine, dillweed, paprika, mushroom soy sauce, sugar, and 1½ teaspoons of the salt. Bring to a boil, then cover and bake for 1½ hours. Stir well and taste for salt and pepper, adding the remaining salt if necessary. Add the optional parsley, if you like.

Serve hot over the Savory Noodle Kugel, and pass Tofu Sour Cream.

Serves 8

Per serving: Calories: 255, Protein: 4 gm., Fat: 0 gm., Carbohydrates: 43 gm.

Savory Noodel Kugel

A kugel is loosely translated as a "pudding." It can be made from grated potatoes and other vegetables or noodles (either sweet or savory), and is usually held together with beaten eggs and/or sour cream and soft cheeses.

This savory kugel is simply made with plain fettucine pasta and a blended tofu mixture with onion and a few other seasonings. It can be made up ahead of time and baked during the last half hour of baking the Vegetable Goulash. When it's golden and crusty on top, cut it into squares to serve with the stew (or serve it as is with a salad as a light supper dish).

Cook the pasta in lots of boiling, salted water until just tender, but not mushy. Drain in a colander. Meanwhile, preheat the oven to 350°F.

Place the tofu, lemon juice, sugar, salt, and cayenne in a food processor (or do it in a blender in two batches), and blend until very smooth. Combine the cooked, drained pasta, all but ½ cup of the blended tofu mixture, the onions, the garlic, and Worcestershire sauce in a large bowl. Mix well and taste for salt. Place in a lightly oiled casserole or 9" x 13" baking pan, smoothing the top. Bake for half an hour, or until golden and crusty on top. Spread the remaining tofu mixture on top, and serve hot.

If you like, you can sprinkle the top with soy parmesan cheese before serving.

Serves 8 to 12

Per serving: Calories: 119, Protein: 9 gm., Fat: 1 gm., Carbohydrates: 19 gm.

---

1 lb. dry fettucine pasta, broken in half

3 (10.5 oz.) pkgs. reduced-fat, firm or
     extra-firm SILKEN tofu,
     or 1½ lbs. reduced-fat, firm or
     medium-firm, regular tofu, crumbled
⅓ c. lemon juice
1½ tsp. sugar or alternate sweetener
1 tsp. salt
dash of cayenne pepper

2 onions, minced
2 cloves garlic, minced or crushed
2 T. Vegetarian Worcestershire Sauce
     (p. 176)

soy parmesan for topping (optional)

Cabbage Strudel

I love this savory strudel (made with phyllo pastry) served with the goulash–it lends a company touch.

½ medium head cabbage, cored and
    thinly shredded
1 medium onion, chopped
2 cloves garlic, minced
1 c. fresh mushrooms, sliced
¾ c. dry white wine
1 tsp. dillweed
½ tsp. salt
freshly ground black pepper to taste

6 full sheets of phyllo pastry, thawed
    and well covered
soymilk for brushing

Tofu Sour Cream for accompaniment
    (p. 174)

To make the filling, steam-fry the cabbage, onions, and garlic in a large, lightly oiled, heavy skillet or pot, until the cabbage starts to wilt. Add the mushrooms and wine, and stir-cook over high heat until the liquid evaporates. Season with the dillweed, salt, and pepper. Spread the filling on a flat dish, and place in the freezer so that it will cool off quickly.

Preheat the oven to 350°F (if you are making the goulash, it will already be on).

Separate and restack the sheets of phyllo pastry on a clean tea towel. Spoon the cabbage filling down one long side of the stack, 2 or 3 inches from the edge. Using the towel as a guide, roll the phyllo and filling up like a jelly roll, lengthwise. Carefully place the roll on a lightly oiled cookie sheet. Brush the roll with soymilk, and bake for about 30 minutes, or until golden. Serve hot, cut into 8 slices, with *Tofu Sour Cream*. This can be made ahead and reheated to crisp it up again.

Serves 8

Per serving: Calories: 97, Protein: 2 gm., Fat: 0 gm., Carbohydrates: 16 gm.

Plum Kuchen

This fruit tart is usually made with a rich cookie crust and a sour cream and egg custard. It's every bit as good—and pretty—when made with our Yeasted Pastry and a creamy tofu topping. You can make it with any fruit, but plums are my favorite.

When the pastry has risen once, preheat the oven to 400°F, and roll the pastry out to fit an oiled, 10" x 15" cookie sheet. Press the dough to fit the pan with a small rim around the edges like a pizza.

Arrange the plum slices in neat rows or an artistic pattern over the pastry. Sprinkle the fruit with the ½ cup sugar or Sucanat, or drizzle with the honey, then sprinkle with the cinnamon. Bake this for 10-15 minutes.

Meanwhile, mix the ingredients for the Creamy Tofu Topping in a blender or food processor until very smooth. Remove the pan from the oven, and drizzle the tofu mixture evenly over the fruit. Smooth it out if necessary. Lower the heat to 375°F, and bake the kuchen for 20 more minutes, or until the tofu mixture is set.

Cool the kuchen in the pan on a rack, and cut it into squares with a very sharp knife. Serve warm or cold.

Serves 8 to 12

Per serving: Calories: 288, Protein: 8 gm., Fat: 2 gm., Carbohydrates: 59 gm.

double recipe of Yeasted Pastry Dough (p. 163)

24 large purple plums, pitted and sliced
½ c. sugar or Sucanat,
    or ⅓ c. honey or alternate sweetener
1 tsp. ground cinnamon

Creamy Tofu Topping
1½ (10.5 oz.) pkgs. reduced-fat, extra-firm SILKEN tofu,
    or ¾ lb. reduced-fat, firm or medium-firm, regular tofu, crumbled
6 T. water
6 T. sugar or Sucanat
2 T. lemon juice
pinch salt

YOM KIPPUR
(Jewish Day of Atonement)
Tishri 10
(10 days after Rosh Hashanah)

MENU

Italian Yom Kippur Bread (Il Bollo—p. 145)

hot coffee, tea, apple juice, or cocoa

Torta
(layered tofu "cream cheese" appetizer
with
Dried Mushroom and Tomato Tappenade)

breadsticks, brittle rye crackers,
raw vegetables, and/or crostini

Pesto Pasta Salad

Potato Kugel

Honey-Glazed Root Vegetables

Hot Fruit Compote

◇◆◇◆◇◆◇◆◇◆◇◆◇◆◇◆◇◆◇◆◇

Yom Kippur Meal

The culmination of the Jewish High Holy Days is Yom Kippur, the Day of Atonement. This is a day of solemnity, when Jews stay home from work and school to fast, pray, and study. Healthy adults fast for most of the day, and after a long religious service, friends and family gather together for a meal to break the fast. This is often like a brunch, consisting of light foods and dairy foods. In North America, coffee and a sweet are often served first, followed by something savory.

This most important holy day of the Jewish calendar comes to an end with a final, long blast of the shofar (ram's horn) at sunset.

Our Yom Kippur "break-fast" starts with a slightly sweet, Italian Yom Kippur Bread (Il Bollo) and hot coffee, tea, juice, or cocoa. An easy, make-ahead buffet meal that crosses cultural borders follows.

This menu would be suitable also for Sukkot (Jewish Harvest Festival), a bar or bat mitzvah or Brit Milah party, or Lammas buffet.

Torta

Layered Tofu "Cream Cheese" Appetizer

with Dried Mushroom and Tomato Tappenade

This impressive, layered mold of Tofu "Cream Cheese" and vegetable spread looks and sounds a bit complicated, but it's actually quite easy and can be made a day or two ahead of serving. It makes an elegant appetizer for any party. Serve it with breadsticks, brittle rye crackers, raw vegetables, and/or crostini (toasted or grilled slices of French or Italian bread). You could also try using Low-fat Pesto, page 95, or your own favorite pesto, tappenade, or colorful, intensely-flavored vegetable spread between the layers of "cream cheese" instead of the following tappenade. A simple mixture of chopped, drained, marinated artichoke hearts (rinse the oil off with hot water), fresh parsley, and roasted red peppers makes a good, quick filling in two layers with three "cream cheese" layers.

The tappenade, a spread usually made with olives but scrumptiously fat-free when made with dried mushrooms and tomatoes, is also delicious by itself on crackers and crostini. (You can double the tappenade recipe to use alone.) The Tofu "Cream Cheese" is also good by itself—halve the recipe if you wish.

To make the tappenade, place the dried mushrooms and tomatoes in separate, small saucepans, and cover with water. Bring them each to a boil, and then simmer for about 10 minutes, or until tender and pliable. Drain them both. Remove the stems of the mushrooms, and discard them. Chop the dried tomatoes.

In a large, heavy skillet, steam-fry the onion, garlic, chopped dried tomatoes, and chopped roasted peppers until the onion begins to get soft. Add the ripe tomato, vinegar, sugar, and oregano, and simmer until the juice evaporates.

Place the mushrooms in the food processor, and chop them finely. Add the contents of the skillet and the salt and pepper to taste. Puree until almost smooth, and refrigerate in a covered container. This makes a little over 1 cup.

(cont.)

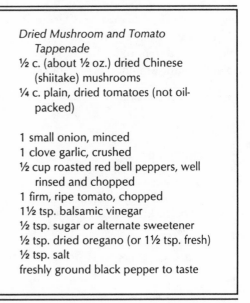

Dried Mushroom and Tomato
  Tappenade
½ c. (about ½ oz.) dried Chinese
  (shiitake) mushrooms
¼ c. plain, dried tomatoes (not oil-
  packed)

1 small onion, minced
1 clove garlic, crushed
½ cup roasted red bell peppers, well
  rinsed and chopped
1 firm, ripe tomato, chopped
1½ tsp. balsamic vinegar
½ tsp. sugar or alternate sweetener
½ tsp. dried oregano (or 1½ tsp. fresh)
½ tsp. salt
freshly ground black pepper to taste

To make the torta, have ready a deep, wide-mouth container which will allow for drainage and will hold about 4 cups of mixture (or use 2 containers which will each hold 2 cups). You can use deep, clean, undyed baskets or flowerpots. A 4-cup round vessel should be about 5" in diameter at the top and 4" deep; a 2-cup round vessel should be about 4" in diameter at the top and 3½" deep, or a square one 3½" across the top and 3½" deep. Line them smoothly with two layers of damp cheesecloth with an overhang of a few inches.

To make the Tofu "Cream Cheese," soak the water and agar in a medium saucepan for 5 minutes. Stir this over low heat until the agar is dissolved, then simmer it gently for 1 minute. Add the crumbled tofu to the pot, and stir it constantly until the tofu is hot to the touch (this is important so that the agar doesn't start firming up *before* the mixture is blended). Pour the hot mixture into a blender or food processor along with the miso, lemon juice, and sugar. Blend or process until it is *very* smooth.

Immediately begin to prepare the torta, while the "cream cheese" is still warm and pourable. Pour ¼ of the "cream cheese" into the prepared container(s). Spoon ⅓ of the tappenade over this, making little "blobs" close together to cover the "cream cheese" right up to the edge (you want the tappenade to show on the edges when you unmold the torta). It's difficult to spread the tappenade over the "cream cheese" when it's soft, so this is the best technique to use. Repeat this layering, ending with the last quarter of the "cream cheese."

Fold the overhang of the cheesecloth over the top of the torta. Set the container(s) on a small rack on a plate, and enclose this in a plastic bag. Refrigerate the torta for several hours or a couple of days, until the "cream cheese" is firmly set and cold.

To serve, carefully fold back the cloth, and invert the torta on a serving plate(s). Remove the container(s), and carefully peel the cloth away. Garnish the torta with herbs, edible flowers, and/or the dippers.

Makes about 4 cups

Per ¼ cup: Calories: 64, Protein: 5 gm., Fat: 2 gm., Carbohydrates: 6 gm.

Tofu "Cream Cheese"
¼ c. cold water
2 tsp. agar powder,
    or ¼ c. agar flakes

2 (10.5 oz.) pkgs. reduced-fat, extra-
    firm, SILKEN tofu, crumbled
2 T. light miso
2 T. lemon juice
1 tsp. sugar, honey, or alternate
    sweetener

Pesto Pasta Salad

Try this delicious, low-fat, vegan pesto on hot pasta, pizza, bruschetta, vegetables, and potatoes as well as this salad—it's amazingly delicious!

ALLERGY NOTE: If you can't eat soy products, try replacing the tofu with ¾ cup well-drained, canned or cooked white beans or dry-mashed potatoes. If you are allergic to wheat, try brown rice rotini from your health food store.

To make the pesto, place all of the pesto ingredients in a food processor or blender, and process until a paste forms. Place in a tightly covered container, and refrigerate until ready to use. (The top may darken a little, but this is just oxidation and doesn't affect the taste—just stir the mixture.) The pesto can be frozen for future use.

Cook the pasta in a large pot of boiling, salted water until just tender. Reserve about a cup of the pasta cooking water. Drain, rinse with cold water, and drain again. Mix the rotini in a large serving bowl with the tomato halves and diced red pepper. Thin the pesto to your taste with the pasta cooking water—it should be like a creamy salad dressing. Toss the salad with the pesto, and taste for salt and pepper. Refrigerate until serving time, but serve at room temperature.

Serves 8 to 10

Per serving: Calories: 102, Protein: 6 gm., Fat: 1 gm., Carbohydrates: 17 gm.

Low-fat Pesto (makes about 1½ c.)
4 c. fresh basil leaves (loosely-packed)
8 cloves garlic, peeled
6 oz. (¾ c.) reduced-fat, firm or
   medium-firm, regular tofu,
   or ½ (10.5 oz.) pkg. reduced-fat,
   extra-firm, SILKEN tofu
¼ c. nutritional yeast flakes,
   or soy parmesan
1½ T. chicken-style vegetarian broth
   powder
1 T. lemon juice
1½ tsp. salt

Salad
1 lb. dry rotini or fusilli pasta
1 lb. cherry tomatoes, rinsed, stemmed,
   and cut in half
1 large red bell pepper, seeded and
   diced

Potato Kugel

A kugel is a type of baked pudding that is very common in Western European Jewish cooking. Kugels can be made from noodles, potatoes, or other vegetables and grains, and can be sweet or savory. This one is particularly easy to make and is somewhat like a giant latke (potato pancake) baked in the oven.

---

2 large onions, peeled and grated or minced
about ½-1 cup vegetarian broth

2 lbs. russet potatoes, scrubbed and grated
2 T. fresh parsley, minced
2 T. powdered egg replacer, whisked to a froth with ½ c. cold vegetarian broth
1 tsp. salt
freshly ground black pepper to taste

Preheat the oven to 400°F. Lightly oil a 9" x 13" baking pan.

Steam-fry the onions in a large, lightly oiled skillet until golden and softened, using vegetarian broth as the liquid. Mix in a large bowl with the grated potatoes, parsley, salt, and pepper. Fold in the beaten egg replacer. Smooth the mixture into the prepared pan, and bake for about 50-60 minutes, or until golden.

Serves 8

Per serving: Calories: 111, Protein: 2 gm., Fat: 0 gm., Carbohydrates: 26 gm.

Honey-Glazed Root Vegetables

This carefree, delectable method for cooking root vegetables is ideal for a crowd, because you can do them in large pans in the oven. The honey can be replaced with maple syrup or fruit concentrate syrup, if you prefer.

Preheat the oven to 400°F. Cut the vegetables into even-sized wedges (about ½" thick and 3" long). Toss them with the marinade and honey, and spread on 2 lightly oiled, shallow baking pans. Bake for 45-60 minutes, turning occasionally, until the vegetables are tender and glazed. Serve hot.

Serves 8

Per serving: Calories: 115, Protein: 1 gm., Fat: 0 gm., Carbohydrates: 26 gm.

2 large carrots, scrubbed or peeled
2 parsnips, peeled
2 medium turnips, peeled
1 rutabaga, peeled
2 large yellow onions, peeled
1 c. Roasting and Grilling Marinade (p. 178)
¼ c. honey

Hot Fruit Compote

Here is a delicious sugar- and honey-free version of a traditional Russian-Jewish fruit compote.

Bring the juice to a boil in a large, non-aluminum saucepan. Add all the other ingredients, except the lemon zest. Bring to a boil, then turn down, cover, and simmer for 30-60 minutes, or until done to your taste. Discard the lemon slices. Serve in bowls with some of the lemon zest sprinkled on top.

Serves 8

Per serving: Calories: 291, Protein: 2 gm., Fat: 0 gm., Carbohydrates: 69 gm.

6 c. apple juice
¾ lb. pitted prunes
½ lb. dried peaches, pears, or apples
½ c. raisins or dried currants
1 cinnamon stick
2-3 whole cloves
one lemon, sliced (grate the zest before slicing)

grated zest of one lemon

THANKSGIVING

4th Thursday in November
in the United States
2nd Monday in October in Canada

MENU
Watercress and Sunchoke Salad
with Cranberry Vinaigrette
Tofu "Turkey"
with Bread or Corn Bread Stuffing
or
Large Squash
with Wild Rice and Chanterelle Stuffing
Maple Baked Beans
or small stuffed squash
Mushroom Gravy
baked sweet potatoes
Green Onion Mashed Potatoes
Cranberry Sauce
Succotash
Hard Rolls (p. 149-50) or Pioneer Corn Bread
Maple Syrup-Granola Tart and/or
Pumpkin Pie (p.165)
with Maple or Vanilla Tofu "Ice Cream"
dry white wine, sparkling wine
(can be non-alcoholic,
or sparkling mineral water)

A Native Thanksgiving

All cultures have festivals of Thanksgiving, and most often they fall around the time of harvest. The First Nations in North America were holding their centuries-old harvest ceremonies and feasts, such as the Iroquois Harvest Ceremony in October or November, long before the Europeans arrived.

On both sides of the U.S./Canadian border, we enjoy many traditional Native American foods today in our homes on Thanksgiving Day. Corn, beans, and squash, often called "the Three Sisters," provide the corn bread or corn bread stuffing, the green beans, and the pumpkin pie or stuffed squash that many of us take for granted will be on our "groaning board" on Thanksgiving. Cranberries, maple syrup, potatoes, and wild mushrooms are other native foods that grace our harvest tables.

To make preparation of this menu easier, many of the dishes can be made ahead, or at least partially made ahead. (Or you can dole out recipes to guests potluck-style.)

There is a choice of main courses: You can try the easy and delicious Tofu "Turkey" and serve small, stuffed squash alongside. Or you can serve a large, wild-rice and mushroom-stuffed squash as a main dish centerpiece, with the Maple Baked Beans and separately baked bread or corn bread stuffing alongside. Colorful squash of all shapes and sizes make a beautiful centerpiece piled in the middle of the table with some Indian corn, and hollowed-out small pumpkins make great dishes for condiments or dips for the meal. The recipes here are for 6 servings, but can be doubled or tripled for crowds.

This feast would also be suitable for a fall wedding or birthday dinner, or an autumn equinox or harvest dinner.

Watercress and Sunchoke Salad
with Cranberry Vinaigrette

Sunchokes are also known as Jerusalem artichokes, but they actually are part of the sunflower family (and native to North America), thus the more modern name. They can be cooked much like potatoes, but they are also delicious raw, with a sweetness and crisp texture reminiscent of fresh water chestnuts. They grow literally like a weed—in fact, you are well advised to grow them in large washtubs so they don't take over the whole garden! Plant them in either fall or spring, and harvest them as you need them the next fall after the stalks have died down. Just leave them right in the ground, and dig them up as needed. Or look for them in good produce markets and health food stores.

To make the cranberry vinaigrette, stir the water or broth and cornstarch together in a small sauce-pan over high heat until it thickens and turns clear. Pour into a blender with the remaining vinaigrette ingredients, and blend until smooth. Place in a cruet or pitcher, and refrigerate until serving time.

To make the salad, scrub and peel the sunchokes, and slice them thinly. You can make one large salad on a platter or individual salads. Either way, line the dish first with the lettuce, then the watercress. Top with the sunchoke slices and onion slices. If made ahead of time, cover well with plastic wrap, and refrigerate until serving time. Drizzle with a little of the cranberry vinaigrette just before serving, and pass the rest.

Serves 6

Per serving: Calories: 83, Protein: 2 gm., Fat: 0 gm., Carbohydrates: 17 gm.

Cranberry Vinaigrette
1 c. cold water or light vegetarian broth
    mixed with 2 tsp. cornstarch
⅓ c. red wine vinegar, cranberry
    vinegar, or balsamic vinegar
¼ c. fresh or thawed, frozen cranber-
    ries, chopped
¼ c. green onion, chopped
2 T. lemon juice
2 cloves garlic
2 tsp. Sesame Meal (p. 175)
2 tsp. salt or herbal salt
freshly ground black pepper to taste
pinch of cayenne pepper

Salad
1 lb. raw sunchokes (get the roundest
    ones you can find, with the least
    knobs, as they are easier to peel)
1 head of buttercrunch or Boston
    lettuce, washed and dried
2 bunches of watercress, washed, dried
    and trimmed
1 medium red or sweet onion, thinly
    sliced

Large or Small Squash
with Wild Rice and Chanterelle Stuffing

If you'd like to make a colorful, stuffed winter squash the centerpiece and main dish of your vegetarian Thanksgiving, choose a large, meaty pumpkin: Boston marrow squash, turban squash, hubbard squash, banana squash, or the pale, blue-grey New Zealand squash, which is my favorite.

For a side dish, stuff hollowed-out halves of acorn, butternut, or buttercup squash, or even small pumpkins.

We pick our own chanterelle mushrooms in the forest near our house, but they are available in good produce stores, supermarkets, and natural food stores. If you can't find them, use fresh shiitakes, oyster mushrooms, or even ordinary mushrooms (the brown ones have more flavor).

3 small winter squash (about 1¼ lb. each),
  or 1 medium-large winter squash (about 6-8 lbs.) (see text for varieties)

Wild Rice and Chanterelle Stuffing
3½ c. light vegetarian broth
1½ c. wild rice

4 c. chanterelles, cleaned and sliced (see text for substitutes)
1 c. green onions, chopped
1 c. onion, minced
4 stalks celery, sliced

½ tsp. dried thyme
½ tsp. dried marjoram
salt and freshly ground black pepper to taste

To precook the squash, cut small squash in half, and scoop out the seeds. Preheat the oven to 350°F. Place the squash halves cut side down in a shallow baking pan with ½" of hot water. Bake for 40 minutes, or just until tender.

For large squash, preheat the oven to 400°F. Cut a "lid" off the top of the squash, and scoop out the seeds, scraping the interior well. Place the squash in a baking pan, with the lid on loosely, and bake for 1 hour, then check for tenderness. If the squash isn't done, cook longer. (It's difficult to be exact with large squash because the cooking time varies with the type of squash and thickness of the flesh.)

To make the stuffing, bring the broth to a boil in a medium pot. Wash the wild rice in a colander under running water. When the water boils, add the washed wild rice, bring to a boil, then cover and turn down to a simmer. Simmer for about 55 minutes, or until tender.

Meanwhile, steam-fry the chanterelles, onions, and celery in a large, nonstick or lightly

oiled skillet until tender and slightly-browned. Add the cooked wild rice, herbs, and salt and pepper to taste.

Mound the stuffing into the large or small squash, and place the squash in a shallow baking pan. (If there is any stuffing left over, place it around the squash.) Cover and bake the small squash at 350°F for 20 minutes, or the large squash for 45-60 minutes. Serve hot with gravy.

Serves 6

Per serving: Calories: 192, Protein: 5 gm., Fat: 1 gm., Carbohydrates: 38 gm.

Mushroom Gravy

T his fat-free and delicious brown gravy is one of my favorite staples–I'll even eat it on toast for breakfast! This version is "gussied up" for a holiday meal. The basic version, from my first book, The Almost No-Fat Cookbook, used only water for the liquid and no mushrooms.

For a giblet-style gravy, add about 1 cup of chopped seitan or prepared textured vegetable protein chunks instead of the mushrooms.

In a large, lightly oiled or nonstick frying pan, steam-fry the mushrooms until tender and slightly browned. Set aside.

In a heavy saucepan over high heat, whisk the yeast and flour together until it smells toasty. Off the heat, whisk in the water, wine, soy sauce, salt, and Kitchen Bouquet, if using. Stir constantly over high heat until it thickens and comes to a boil. Reduce the heat and simmer for 2-5 minutes. This can be made ahead and reheated.

Makes about 2½ cups

Per ¼ cup: Calories: 70, Protein: 3 gm., Fat: 0 gm., Carbohydrates: 7 gm.

4 c. fresh mushrooms (any kind), sliced
⅓ c. unbleached flour
⅓ c. nutritional yeast flakes
1½ c. water
1 c. dry white wine
2 T. soy sauce or mushroom soy sauce
½ tsp. salt
a few shakes of Kitchen Bouquet, or other gravy browner (optional)

Tofu "Turkey"

with Bread or Corn Bread Stuffing

T his doesn't really look like a turkey (it's square), but that wasn't my intention. It does have a taste and texture quite similar to turkey breast with crispy skin and a moist stuffing layered in between. You can use your own favorite stuffing, if you prefer. If you're making corn bread stuffing, be sure to make the corn bread several days ahead of time (see recipe on page 107).

As long as you've marinated the tofu for several days, this dish is easy and fast to put together (in fact, you can assemble it the day before you cook it), and it's tasty when cold too. I like it any time of the year! The only really unusual ingredient needed for this recipe is dried Chinese bean curd sheets (called "yuba" in Japanese). They can be found in Asian grocery stores, some health food stores, and large supermarkets. This product is simply the "skin" that forms on the top of soymilk when it is heated (just as it does with ordinary milk). The "skin" is lifted off and dried, and is considered a delicacy in Chinese and Japanese cuisine. In its dried form, it keeps for a long time, as long as it is stored airtight. When reconstituted, wrapped around tofu or other fillings, and baked, it becomes delicately crispy.

1½-2 lbs. reduced-fat, extra-firm or
    pressed, regular tofu

Tofu Marinade
3 c. water
½ c. soy sauce
6 T. nutritional yeast flakes
4 tsp. dried sage leaves, crumbled
1 tsp. onion powder
1 tsp. dried thyme
1 tsp. dried rosemary

2 sheets of dried Chinese bean curd
    skin

The day before or several days before cooking, slice the tofu into 5 long slabs per pound. Combine the marinade ingredients and place the tofu with the marinade to cover in a covered container. Refrigerate until you use it, shaking or stirring occasionally.

Soak the dried bean curd skin in warm water to cover while you make the stuffing.

To make the stuffing, steam-fry the onion and celery in a large, lightly oiled or nonstick frying pan until softened. Remove from heat and add the remaining stuffing ingredients. Mix well.

To assemble the "turkey" (which can be done the day before cooking), oil a 9" x 9" square baking pan with the Chinese sesame oil. Line the bottom and sides with the soaked bean curd skin, leaving an overhang.

Cut one third of the marinated tofu to fit the bottom of the pan. Top this layer of tofu with half of the stuffing. Cut another third of the tofu to fit over that. Top with the remaining stuffing. Cut the last of the tofu to fit, and place it over the stuffing. Fold the overhanging bean curd skin over the casserole. If made ahead, cover the casserole and refrigerate until baking time.

Preheat the oven to 350°F. Bake the casserole, uncovered, for 1 hour. Loosen the edges carefully and invert it onto a serving plate. To serve, cut into 8 pieces and accompany with Mushroom Gravy and cranberry sauce.

Stuffing Variations: Everyone has very personal likes and dislikes when it comes to stuffing. Obviously, I like a basic sage and onion one with celery and other herbs. Feel free to add your favorite ingredients. Here are some suggestions: chopped fresh parsley or other fresh herbs; soy bacon bits; chopped apples, cranberries, or pears; dried fruit; vegetarian sausage; chestnuts; a bit of brandy, whiskey, or wine in place of some of the broth; some cooked wild rice (see recipe p. 100) in place of some of the bread; steam-fried mushrooms (any kind)—if you used to be fond of oyster stuffing, use oyster mushrooms and maybe a bit of Chinese vegetarian "oyster" sauce (which is made with mushrooms, but tastes quite "oystery").

Serves 8

Per serving: Calories: 190, Protein: 17 gm., Fat: 5 gm., Carbohydrates: 18 gm.

Stuffing
1 large onion, chopped
1 c. celery and tops, chopped
4 c. fresh whole wheat bread or corn bread cubes
1 c. vegetarian broth
about ½ tsp. EACH of dried sage, thyme, and savory or to taste
pinch of dried rosemary
salt and freshly ground black pepper to taste (you won't need salt if the broth is salted)

Chinese sesame oil for oiling the pan

Baked Stuffing

To bake the stuffing as a separate dish, double the recipe and pack it in a prepared pan without the tofu and bean curd skin. Lightly brush the top with Chinese sesame oil, cover with foil, and bake at 350°F for 30-60 minutes (depending on how crusty you like it).

Maple Baked Beans

Two Native American ingredients, maple syrup and anasazi beans (which do not cause the same gastric distress that many dried beans do), make this a delectable main dish, sure to be a family favorite all year long.

---

2 c. dried anasazi beans (or, if you can't find them, use small, white navy or pea beans, or pintos)

2 T. Sesame Meal (p. 175)
1 small onion, peeled
1 c. pure maple syrup (grade B is the best for this recipe)
2 tsp. salt
1 tsp. dry mustard

Soak the beans in water to cover overnight or for 8 hours. Drain the soaking water off, and cover the beans with 6 cups fresh water in a large pot. Bring this to a boil, then lower the heat and simmer for 10 minutes. Drain the beans and reserve the cooking water. Preheat the oven to 300°F.

Place the beans in a casserole or bean pot, and mix with the Sesame Meal. Insert the onion in the center. Mix the maple syrup with ¾ cup of the reserved bean liquid, the salt, and dry mustard. Pour over the beans. Add just enough bean liquid to cover the beans. Cover the pot and bake for 2 hours. Add the remaining bean liquid, stir well, and bake for 1½ to 2 hours more, or until the beans are very soft and the liquid is absorbed (uncover for the last half hour or so). Adjust sweetness to taste. Serve hot.

Slow-Cooker Method: Cook the soaked beans for 40-60 minutes, or until the beans are tender. Chop the onion instead of leaving it whole. Use only ¾ cup of the reserved bean liquid (slow-cookers do not evaporate liquid as oven-baking does). Cook on high for 5-6 hours, or on low for 10-12 hours.

Serves 6

Per serving: Calories: 321, Protein: 11 gm., Fat: 0 gm., Carbohydrates: 67 gm.

Green Onion Mashed Potatoes

I don't care how elegant the meal, I want mashed potatoes to go with my gravy! Without the green onions, this is a good, basic recipe to follow for making well-seasoned mashed potatoes without butter and milk or cream.

Boil the potatoes in water to cover until tender. Drain them and mash in the pot. Beat in the soymilk (or alternate) and green onions, and season with salt and pepper to taste. Serve hot with Mushroom Gravy or other gravy.

Leftovers are delicious made into little "cakes" and browned over medium heat in a heavy, lightly oiled or nonstick skillet.

Serves 6

Per serving: Calories: 247, Protein: 4 gm., Fat: 1 gm., Carbohydrates: 56 gm.

12 medium russet potatoes, peeled and cut into even chunks
1 c. plain soymilk (you can use reduced-fat, but regular soymilk is a bit richer),
    or 1 c. other non-dairy "milk,"
    or 1 c. Tofu Sour Cream (p. 174)
1 c. green onions, minced
salt and white pepper to taste

Cranberry Sauce

I always like to make my own cranberry sauce instead of using canned, and it's one of the easiest parts of a holiday dinner to make, especially since it can be made several days ahead.

1 (12 oz.) pkg. fresh cranberries, rinsed, sorted and trimmed
1 c. cranberry juice cocktail, or a cranberry and fruit juice mix (like cran-apple or cranberry-raspberry)
½ c. sugar, turbinado sugar, or Sucanat

Combine the ingredients in a large, heavy, non-aluminum saucepan, and bring to a boil. Turn the heat to medium, and cook about 10 minutes, or until the cranberries have popped open; skim off any foam. Cool and place the sauce in a serving dish. Cover and refrigerate until serving time.

You may substitute 1 cup maple syrup for the sugar or add ½ teaspoon maple flavoring.

Serves 10 to 12 as a condiment

Per serving: Calories: 60, Protein: 0 gm., Fat: 0 gm., Carbohydrates: 15 gm.

Succotash

There are many variations on succotash, a favorite, American bean and corn dish that originated with the First Nations tribes of the northeastern United States and southeastern Canada. Modern succotash recipes often call for cream, but I prefer a version more like the original.

1 (10 oz.) pkg. frozen baby lima beans
1 (10 oz.) pkg. frozen, whole, small green beans
2 c. fresh or frozen corn kernels
1½ c. light vegetarian broth
1 c. green onions, chopped
1 green bell pepper, seeded and diced
1 red bell pepper, seeded and diced
1 tsp. cornstarch dissolved in 1 T. cold water
salt and freshly ground black pepper to taste

Place the lima beans, green beans, and corn in a medium saucepan with the broth. Cover and bring to a boil. Reduce heat to medium-low, and simmer for 10 minutes. Add the green onions and peppers, and simmer 5 minutes more. Remove the cover and cook over high heat for 4-5 minutes, or until the liquid is reduced to about ½ cup. Stir in the dissolved cornstarch, and stir until it thickens and clears. Taste for salt and pepper, and serve immediately.

Serves 6

Per serving: Calories: 118, Protein: 5 gm., Fat: 0 gm., Carbohydrates: 24 gm.

Pioneer Corn Bread

T his is a slightly modernized version of an old Kentucky recipe for plain corn bread. Eat it as a hot bread, or leave it for a few days and use it for the stuffing.

Preheat the oven to 350°F. Lightly oil two 8" round cake pans or cast iron skillets, and place in the oven while it heats up. (If you pour corn bread batter into hot pans, especially heavy skillets, it gets a crispier crust).

Mix the cornmeal, flour, sugar, nutritional yeast, baking soda, and salt in a medium bowl. In a large measuring cup, mix together the soymilk and lemon juice—it will curdle slightly and look like buttermilk. In a small, deep bowl, beat the egg replacer and water with an electric hand mixer, or whisk until like softly mounded beaten egg whites.

Stir the soymilk into the dry ingredients, and mix briefly with a fork—a few lumps are fine. Carefully fold in the beaten egg replacer until evenly distributed.

Pour the batter into the hot pans, and bake for about 30 minutes, or until they test done in the center.

Makes two 8" round corn breads (8 servings)

Per serving: Calories: 170, Protein: 5 gm., Fat: 1 gm., Carbohydrates: 36 gm.

1 c. yellow cornmeal
1 c. unbleached flour
⅓ c. sugar or alternate sweetener
2 T. nutritional yeast flakes
1 tsp. baking soda
½ tsp. salt

2 c. reduced-fat soymilk
2 T. lemon juice

1 T. powdered egg replacer beaten with
 ¼ c. cold water

Maple Syrup-Granola Tart

This tart uses the Low-fat Oil Pastry on page 161, which is the only recipe in this book that calls for any added oil. I've included it because some holiday pie and tart recipes just don't taste right with the Yeasted Pastry Dough. However, even with the pastry, one slice of the tart contains only 5 grams of fat because the filling contains no fat! This is a beautiful dessert as well as delicious, with a sparkling amber color. You'll be proud to serve it.

This recipe first appeared in the November 1994 issue of Vegetarian Times.

---

1 9" crust Low-fat Oil Pastry, uncooked
   (p. 161)
⅔ c. No-Oil Granola (p. 179)

Maple Filling
1 c. pure maple syrup (preferably grade B)
½ c. water
4 T. cornstarch dissolved in 3 T. cold
   water
½ tsp. pure vanilla extract

Line a 9" tart pan or shallow pie pan with the pastry. (If using a pie pan, trim the pastry right at the inside top edge of the pan, not the outside edge.)

Preheat the oven to 400°F.

In a small saucepan, mix together the maple syrup and water. Let it boil for 5 minutes. Whisk in the dissolved cornstarch, and continue to whisk over high heat until it becomes thick and clear. Stir in the vanilla and set aside.

Sprinkle the granola over the bottom of the crust. Pour the maple syrup mixture over this, and spread it evenly. Place the tart in the center of the oven, and immediately reduce the heat to 350°F. Bake for 30 minutes, then cool thoroughly on a rack before serving.

Serves 8

Per serving: Calories: 243, Protein: 3 gm., Fat: 5 gm., Carbohydrates: 45 gm.

Hannukah Buffet

Although Hannukah is probably the best-known Jewish holiday to non-Jews, it is not a Jewish High Holy Day. It is a delightful holiday—eight days of songs, games, candles, small gifts, and delicious foods. But it is also a celebration of the first great victory for religious freedom, which saved the Jews from extinction.

The legend tells us that Judah Maccabee (who with his father triumphed over the Syrian-Greeks who had desecrated the Temple in Jerusalem) could not find enough holy oil to keep the menorah burning to rededicate the Temple. Only one tiny bottle, enough for one day, was found. But a miracle happened and the lamp kept burning for eight nights! (In memory of this miraculous oil, oily foods are traditional at Hannukah.)

Hannukah candles symbolize spirit, courage, justice, and hope. The hanukkiyyah, the Hannukah menorah or candelabra, has eight places and a ninth one for the shammash, or "servant" candle which lights the others. The candles are lit at nightfall, one more candle each night, with two blessings being said.

With eight days of festivities, there are many opportunities for get-togethers and feasting. Playing games has been a popular Hannukah tradition—puzzles and kattoves (number puzzles), cards, chess, and the dreidel, a spinning top. It has been traditional to give teachers, students, and children coins, or *gelt*, for Hannukah, but now many people exchange small gifts.

We can enjoy many traditional Hannukah foods, such as latkes (potato pancakes), without oil. Many Jewish families make gingerbread cookies at Hannukah, even though it is more traditional to do so during the festival of Purim. Carob brownies also seem appropriate here, as children in the old days used to nibble carob while spinning dreidels.

This menu could also be used for a bar or bat mitzvah or Brit Milah party.

HANNUKAH
(Jewish Feast of Dedication or Festival of Lights)

8 days beginning on 25 Kislev, around the time of the winter solstice

MENU

Potato Latkes (pancakes)
with applesauce and
Tofu Sour Cream (p. 174)

Mock Chopped Liver
with brittle rye crackers
or rye bread toast

Green Bean Stroganoff
over cooked linguine or fettucine noodles

Ginger Crinkles (p. 159)

Almost No-Fat Carob Brownies (p. 157)

hot spiced apple cider

Potato Latkes

I could eat latkes every day of the week! This recipe makes delicious latkes even without the eggs and oil. For other occasions, try them with cranberry sauce, or even ketchup. They are great for breakfast or any meal of the day.

---

9 medium russet potatoes, peeled and grated
1 large onion, peeled and grated
¾ c. whole wheat flour
⅓ c. nutritional yeast flakes
1 T. baking powder
1½ tsp. salt
¼ tsp. white pepper

Mix the onion and potato together well in a large bowl. Add the other ingredients and mix well.

You can cook these on several large, heavy skillets (nonstick or lightly oiled) over medium-high heat, but the easiest way is to use a nonstick, electric pancake griddle–this accommodates quite a few latkes, and they cook evenly. Place ¼ cup of the potato mixture for each latke onto the preheated griddle or skillets, and flatten into thin pancakes with a spatula. Cover them with lids or foil (I use inverted cookie sheets over the griddle) until the bottoms are golden-brown. Then flip them over and cook, uncovered, until the second side is golden-brown. Serve hot with applesauce and Tofu Sour Cream (p. 174).

Serves 6 (makes about 30 pancakes)

Per latke: Calories: 51, Protein: 1 gm., Fat: 0 gm., Carbohydrates: 11 gm.

Variations: You can use ½ potato and ½ carrot, yam, turnip, parsnip, zucchini, or winter squash, or some grated broccoli stem (peeled) or radish in place of some of the potato, along with the onion. Add some dried dillweed, if you like. You can also add some crushed garlic and/or dried herbs, caraway seeds, or chives, or Indian herbs and spices, such as cumin and turmeric.

Mock Chopped Liver

Since observant Jews are not supposed to eat meat and dairy foods together, many versions of mock chopped liver appear in Jewish dairy restaurants. Many are made with nuts. This one, adapted from a recipe in Debra Wasserman's The Lowfat Jewish Vegetarian Cookbook (see page 185), replaces nuts with dry-roasted soybeans or chickpeas.

Cook the baby limas in water to cover for about 10 minutes, or until tender. Drain, reserving ¼ cup of the cooking water.

In a medium, nonstick or lightly oiled pan, steam-fry the mushrooms, onions, and garlic until the onion is tender.

Place the cooked limas, mushroom mixture, reserved cooking water, and other ingredients in a food processor, and process until very smooth. Pile into a serving bowl, and chill the mixture until serving time.

Serves 6

Per serving: Calories: 72, Protein: 4 gm., Fat: 0 gm., Carbohydrates: 12 gm.

8 oz. frozen baby lima beans

¾ lb. fresh mushrooms, chopped
1 small onion, minced
2 cloves garlic, crushed

¼ c. lima bean cooking water
¼ c. Dry-Roasted Soybeans or Chickpeas (p. 176)
1 tsp. salt
black pepper to taste

Green Bean Stroganoff

T he original of this deliciously simple recipe was given to me many years ago by Judy Savage, who keeps a kosher kitchen in Northford, Connecticut. Frozen, whole, small green beans work well during the winter season. Serve over regular pasta, broken in half before cooking, instead of the traditional egg noodles, as it contains no egg.

3 large onions, thinly sliced
2 cloves garlic, minced
⅓ c. dry white wine

1½ lbs. frozen or fresh, whole, small green beans
¾ lb. fresh mushrooms, sliced
1 T. dried basil (or 3 T. fresh, chopped)

1 (10.5 oz). pkg. reduced-fat, firm, SILKEN tofu
⅓ c. water
⅓ c. soy sauce or tamari
2½ T. lemon juice
¼ tsp. sugar or alternate sweetener

salt and freshly ground black pepper to taste

Heat a large, heavy, nonstick or lightly oiled skillet, over high heat. Add the onions and garlic, and steam-fry with 3 tablespoons of the wine until the onion starts to soften (using a little water if necessary). Add the green beans, mushrooms, basil, and remaining wine. Cover and cook over medium heat for 5 minutes, or until the beans are done to your liking.

Meanwhile, mix the tofu, water, soy sauce, lemon juice, and sugar in a blender or food processor until very smooth. Pour this into the pan with the vegetables. Turn the heat to low, and heat the mixture gently. Taste for salt and pepper. Serve hot over hot, cooked linguine or fettucine noodles.

Serves 6

Per serving: Calories: 154, Protein: 10 gm., Fat: 2 gm., Carbohydrates: 19 gm.

Christmas Morning Brunch and Christmas Country Dinner

Many of us bring Christmas traditions from our parents and their family backgrounds when we start our own families. If we are part of a couple, our partner also brings traditions along. Unless both come from the same ethnic and religious background, there will be some compromising and new traditions created. If one or more of the family is a vegetarian (a much more common occurrence these days), new culinary traditions must be found as well.

If you have a mixed ethnic background, as I do, you might like to choose what appeals to you from the different traditions in your family. For instance, I always make panettone, an Italian Christmas bread that my paternal grandmother from Genoa served (her mother made it in a brick oven), except that I make my own low-fat, vegan version. I make a vegetarian tourtière (a "meat" pie) now, since my husband is from Quebec, where this is traditional. Our Christmas dinner is traditionally North American (cranberry sauce, mashed potatoes, sweet potatoes, gravy, etc.), since my mother and I were born in the U.S. and now live in Canada, but I now make a vegetarian main dish.

Christmas is a festival so rich in history, folklore, symbolism, and religious and ethnic tradition that I cannot even begin to delve into anything except Christmas food in this book (see the bibliography for books on the subject if you are as fascinated as I am). Indeed, no Christian holiday (except perhaps Easter) has more symbolic foods than Christmas. Many of these are breads and desserts.

Grain has been a symbol of fertility, good fortune, and plenty since the dawn of time, and breads

CHRISTMAS
December 25

CHRISTMAS MORNING BRUNCH MENU

Panettone (p. 147)
or other favorite Christmas bread

Vegetarian Tourtière (Quebec "meat" pie)
or
Vegetarian Scrapple

Mushroom Gravy (p. 101),

ketchup, chutney, relish
apples, pears, mandarin oranges,
or other fresh fruit

Hot Fruit Compote (p. 97)
and/or
applesauce

hot beverages
(coffee, tea, apple cider,
or Hot Chocolate, p. 18)

Vegan Eggnog

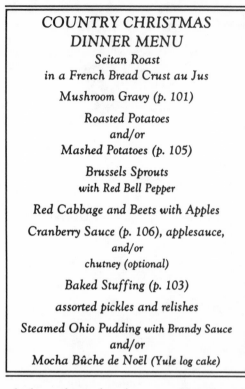

COUNTRY CHRISTMAS DINNER MENU

Seitan Roast
in a French Bread Crust au Jus

Mushroom Gravy (p. 101)

Roasted Potatoes
and/or
Mashed Potatoes (p. 105)

Brussels Sprouts
with Red Bell Pepper

Red Cabbage and Beets with Apples

Cranberry Sauce (p. 106), applesauce,
and/or
chutney (optional)

Baked Stuffing (p. 103)

assorted pickles and relishes

Steamed Ohio Pudding with Brandy Sauce
and/or
Mocha Bûche de Noël (Yule log cake)

are still used symbolically. Christmas, like the pagan winter celebrations that preceded and influenced it, and like the winter festivals of many other religions, celebrates the triumph of light over darkness (physically and spiritually), and hope amid despair. Holiday breads and sweets reflect this. For instance, Scottish shortbread is the modern equivalent of the Celtic oat bannock served at Yule celebrations. It is still often baked as a round cake with a circle in the middle and raised ridges around the rim to signify the rays of the sun that everyone prayed fervently would return again.

Plum pudding was sacred to the Druids, and German springerle cookies were originally made (probably in a less rich and sweet version) to honor the Norse God Wotan and his horse (which you can still see pictured in some of the springerle molds). The Bûche de Noël, or Yule log cake which is popular in many European countries, harkens back to the Viking Yule log which was burned to chase away King Frost. In North America, we leave cookies for our special old Christmas elf, Santa Claus.

The original of the traditional, Christmas cake "log," a sponge cake roll with rum and a mocha-flavored butter cream icing, is France's most famous holiday specialty. Virtually the same cake is served in Northern Italy and called Ceppo di Natale. In Lithuania, a similar cake roll, called a Birch Log, is filled with a prune, nut, and chocolate filling and iced with fondant and chocolate icing. In England, the filling is often apricot jam and almonds, and the roll is first spread with red currant jelly, then almond paste, then a chocolate icing. In Norway, the orange-flavored cake is spread with raspberry or strawberry jam and iced with whipped cream or almond paste icing, with chocolate icing on the ends.

For the country-style, vegetarian Christmas dinner, the centerpiece is a rich-tasting seitan roast (made ahead of time) baked in a golden, French bread crust. (If you prefer, you can use the giant, wild rice- and mushroom-stuffed squash or the Tofu "Turkey" from the Thanksgiving dinner menu instead, or the Tofu Pot Pie from my first cookbook, *The Almost No-Fat Cookbook*, for the main dish.)

This menu could be used for a Réveillon (Christmas Eve) or Yule dinner, or for a winter wedding, anniversary, or birthday celebration.

Vegetarian Tourtière
Quebec "Meat" Pie

My husband Brian, though not French-Canadian, was born in Quebec, and he was so happy when I came up with a vegetarian version of tourtière. It's an integral part of Canadian Christmas celebrations now, and I have seen several recipes for vegetarian versions, using millet, tofu, mushrooms, etc. in the filling. Now you can even buy frozen, vegetarian tourtière all over Canada.

My recipe is made with a fat-free filling of ground seitan with potatoes, onion, and herbs. You can use a single or double Low-Fat Oil Pastry crust (double is traditional, but will also double the fat count!), or the fat-free Yeasted Pastry Dough. Either way, tourtière is traditionally eaten at any meal, hot or cold, with gravy, relish, chutney, or ketchup (although some members of our family have been known to eat it with hot sauce or salsa!). Tourtière is good any time of the year and makes good picnic fare.

Preheat the oven to 350°F.

In a large, nonstick or lightly oiled, heavy skillet, steam-fry the onions and garlic until soft. Place the onions in a large bowl along with the ground seitan, hot water with Marmite, ketchup, and seasonings. Add the potatoes and mix well.

If you are making a double-crust pie, line a 9" pie dish with half of the pastry, and fill with the seitan filling. Otherwise, just press the filling into a nonstick or lightly oiled pie dish. Cover with the remaining pastry, and trim and flute the edges. Cut slits in the top, and brush with soymilk. Bake for 50 minutes.

Serves 8

Per serving: Calories: 273, Protein: 33 gm., Fat: 1 gm., Carbohydrates: 33 gm.

single or double crust of Yeasted Pastry Dough (p. 163)
    or Low-Fat Oil Pastry (p. 161),
soymilk for brushing

Filling
1 large onion, minced
2 large cloves garlic, minced,
    or ½ tsp. garlic granules

1 lb. of Beefy Seitan Roast (p. 173),
    ground in a food processor or grinder
½ c. hot water mixed with 2 tsp. yeast
    extract (Marmite)
2 T. ketchup
1½ tsp. dried savory
½ tsp. celery seed
¼ tsp. ground allspice

½ lb. russet potatoes, peeled, boiled and
    coarsely mashed,
    or 1 c. instant mashed potato flakes
    mixed with ⅔ c. boiling water

Vegetarian Scrapple

S crapple is an old Pennsylvania Dutch or Mennonite dish made from yellow cornmeal mush with pork scraps and herbs. It is chilled and sliced like Italian polenta, then fried and served with syrup, gravy, or applesauce as a breakfast dish. My version uses vegetarian sausage for a delicious, down-home breakfast or supper dish which feels hearty, but is actually almost-no-fat!

Make the scrapple loaf several days ahead of time, then slice it and brown it at the last minute. Serve it with applesauce, maple syrup, ketchup, or a simple version of the gravy on page 101, made with water instead of wine.

1½ c. yellow cornmeal
1 c. cold water
4 vegetarian bouillon cubes dissolved in
   3 c. boiling water
1 tsp. salt if the bouillon is unsalted
   (optional)
¼ tsp. freshly ground black pepper
¼ tsp. dried sage, crumbled
¼ tsp. dried savory

1 c. carrot, grated,
   1 apple, chopped,
   1 stalk celery, minced,
   and/or 1 medium onion, minced or
   grated (optional)

2 c. cooked Vegetarian "Sausage"
   (p. 171), crumbled, or commercial,
   low-fat, vegetarian sausage, cooked

unbleached flour for dredging

Mix the cornmeal and cold water together in a heavy pot. Slowly add the hot bouillon (and salt, if using), along with the herbs. (If you are using the optional grated or minced vegetables or apples, add them now.) Bring this to a boil, stirring with a heavy, wooden spoon. Turn the heat down, cover, and cook until thickened (about 20 minutes), stirring occasionally.

When the cornmeal mush is thick, add the crumbled sausage, and stir until well distributed. Pour this into a nonstick or lightly oiled, 9" x 5" loaf pan, cover, and refrigerate overnight, or for several days.

When ready to cook, slice the loaf ½" thick, and dredge in flour. Brown the slices on both sides on a nonstick or lightly oiled, heavy frying pan or griddle (an electric pancake griddle works well) over medium heat. Turn the slices carefully. When they are crispy on the outside, serve with hot applesauce, gravy, maple syrup, or ketchup.

Serves 8

Per serving: Calories: 163, Protein: 12 gm., Fat: 1 gm., Carbohydrates: 26 gm.

Vegan Eggnog

This "eggnog" will please even those who say they don't like soymilk. It's not too thick and cloying—a very refreshing drink any time of the year. Make the eggnog mix ahead of time, then blend with the ice cubes just before serving.

Place the crumbled tofu and the soymilk in a blender with the sugar and salt. Blend until *very* smooth. Scrape this into a large bowl or pitcher, and whisk in the water, rum or brandy, and vanilla. Mix well, cover, and refrigerate until serving time.

To serve, blend half of the mixture in the blender with 10 of the ice cubes until frothy. Repeat with the other half. Serve in glasses with nutmeg sprinkled on top.

Serves 10

Per serving: Calories: 130, Protein: 5 gm., Fat: 1 gm., Carbohydrates: 13 gm.

2 (10.5 oz.) pkgs. reduced-fat, extra-firm, SILKEN tofu
2 c. reduced-fat soymilk, or other plain, non-dairy "milk"
⅔ c. turbinado sugar, light brown sugar, or Sucanat (or use ½ c. honey or 1 c. alternate liquid sweetener)
¼ tsp. salt

1 c. cold water
1 c. rum or brandy (or use apple juice with rum or brandy flavoring to taste)
4½ tsp. pure vanilla extract

20 ice cubes
freshly grated nutmeg

Seitan Roast
in a French Bread Crust au Jus

This juicy, herb-scented seitan roast in a crusty French bread "basket" will be the hit of a company dinner. The roast can be made, sliced, and reassembled several days ahead of time, and the bread dough can be made the day before and refrigerated.

The crusty bread is perfect to soak up the tasty seitan broth—much better than the greasy pastry crusts that are the usual wraps for elegant loaves and roasts. Serve gravy (page 101) as well, for those who prefer it.

---

1 Beefy Seitan Roast (p. 173), made one to several days ahead and refrigerated, covered, in its cooking broth
1 recipe French Bread dough (pgs. 149-50) made up to 24 hours ahead and refrigerated, well covered in plastic
1 recipe Starch Glaze for Bread (p. 142)

Herb Mixture
6 cloves garlic, minced
½ c. fresh parsley, minced
1½ tsp. dried sage, crumbled
1½ tsp. dried rosemary, basil or other favorite herb
¼ tsp. freshly ground black pepper

Two to three hours before serving, remove the Beefy Seitan Roast and the French bread dough from the refrigerator. Slice the roast neatly into thin slices, then reassemble the roast, and wrap white string around it like a package to hold the slices in place so that it looks like a roast shape again. Reserve the broth.

Using a tape measure, measure the circumference of the roast at the thickest point and the length at the longest point, and jot those numbers down.

Punch the dough down, turn it out on a lightly-floured surface, and roll it out into a rectangle ¼" thick. Cut the rectangle 2" wider than the roast's circumference and 3" longer than its length. Place any dough trimmings in a plastic bag, and refrigerate until later.

Spread half of the herb mixture down the center of the dough rectangle in a strip about the width of the roast. Place the reassembled roast down on this mixture. Spread the remaining herb mixture over the top of the roast. Brush water all around the edges of the dough, and fold the sides of the dough up over the roast so that the edges overlap slightly in the middle. Press the edges together. Fold in the ends and seal them.

Place the roast, seam side down, on a lightly oiled, shallow baking pan. Let the roast stand, lightly covered, in a warm place until the dough is puffy, 30 to 60 minutes. Meanwhile, make the Starch Glaze, and set aside.

If you like, form the dough trimmings into 2" balls, then flatten them out into 5" or 6" rounds. Cover them loosely and let them stand in a warm place until puffy, then brush them with the Starch Glaze, and sprinkle with garlic salt or herbs. Bake them on a cookie sheet alongside the roast for about 20 minutes, or until golden. Serve warm with the roast, or save for another meal.

Preheat the oven to 375°F. When the dough is ready, prick it with a fork around the sides in 3 or 4 places. Brush with the Starch Glaze, and bake 15 minutes. Brush again and bake 35-40 minutes longer, or until the crust is golden brown.

Meanwhile, combine the reserved seitan broth with water if it is too strong (you can use dry wine to replace some of it, if you like). You might need as much as ½ cup water to each ¾ cup broth. Heat this before serving (if you use wine, boil it for a few minutes to cook off the alcohol).

To serve, cut the top off the bread "basket" with a serrated knife, cut the string, and pull string out. Lift out the seitan slices, cutting or breaking off pieces of bread with each serving. Pass the broth (and gravy, if desired) to serve with the roast and bread.

Serves 8

Per serving: Calories: 316, Protein: 36 gm., Fat: 1 gm., Carbohydrates: 40 gm.

Roasted Potatoes

Nothing is more delightful with any sort of roast than crispy, oven-roasted potatoes. Unfortunately, they are usually covered with oil, shortening, or meat drippings. With the versatile Roasting and Grilling Marinade on page 178, however, you can enjoy crispy, roasted potatoes on holidays or any day.

These can be made a few hours ahead of time, then piled in one big pan to reheat for half an hour or so, if you don't have a lot of oven space (or you can opt for the mashed potatoes).

16 medium potatoes (your favorite kind), scrubbed and sliced into wedges or "chips"
1 recipe Roasting and Grilling Marinade (p. 178)
about 3 T. dried herbs of choice (optional)

Preheat the oven to 400°F. Toss the potatoes with about 2½ cups of the marinade, and the optional herbs, if desired. Spread the potatoes on four large, dark cookie sheets (nonstick or lightly oiled), and sprinkle them with salt. Bake for about 1 hour, loosening them with a spatula and turning them from time to time. Move the cookie sheets from the top rack to the bottom and vice versa halfway through.

If you only have room for two pans, cook two batches, then pile them all on one large or two smaller pans, and reheat them to serve.

Serves 8

Per serving: Calories: 247, Protein: 3 gm., Fat: 0 gm., Carbohydrates: 58 gm.

Brussels Sprouts
with Red Peppers

B russels sprouts are a traditional vegetable for Christmas dinner in countries with a large population of English ancestry. If you think of Brussels sprouts as soggy little heads of gray-green cabbage, you've only had over-cooked Brussels sprouts. In actuality, these little, bright green sprouts, when cooked only briefly (or used raw, cut in half, as crudites), are crispy, tasty, and beautiful! Paired with bright, red bell peppers, they make a gorgeous holiday vegetable dish.

If cooking the sprouts whole, cut little crosshatches in the stems to promote even cooking. I like to steam-fry or stir-fry them, cut in halves or quarters. This preserves their crisp texture and bright green color better than steaming. (By the way, sprouts stay bright green when microwaved.)

Have everything ready and quickly cook this dish at the last minute.

Heat a large, nonstick or lightly oiled skillet or wok over high heat. Add the Brussels sprouts, garlic, and a few drops of broth, and stir-fry briefly. Add the peppers and remaining broth, and stir-fry over high heat, uncovered, for 2 minutes. Cover and cook for 1 minute. Add the green onions, salt, and pepper to taste, and stir-fry briefly just to heat. Pour into a warm serving bowl, and serve immediately.

Serves 8

2 lbs. fresh, trimmed Brussels sprouts, quartered
4 cloves garlic, minced
1 c. vegetarian broth

3 c. red bell pepper, sliced

1 c. green onions, sliced
salt and freshly ground black pepper to taste

Per serving: Calories: 52 , Protein: 2 gm., Fat: 0 gm., Carbohydrates: 10 gm.

Red Cabbage and Beets
with Apples

*T*his *is another beautiful and delicious winter vegetable dish that is perfect for a holiday dinner. Like Brussels Sprouts and Red Peppers, it requires very little time, but should be made at the last minute.*

6 c. (about 1¼ lb.) red cabbage, shredded
1½ c. raw beets (about 6 oz.), peeled and shredded
1 medium onion, thinly sliced

1 large apple, grated
⅓ c. apple cider vinegar
2 T. Sucanat or brown sugar
¼ tsp. ground allspice
salt and freshly ground black pepper to taste

In a large, nonstick or lightly oiled skillet or wok, steam-fry the cabbage, beets, and onions, using a little bit of water or broth just to keep from sticking. Stir-fry for 2 or 3 minutes, just until the cabbage begins to wilt.

Add the apple, vinegar, sugar, and allspice. Stir-fry about 1 minute, or until the apples are hot. Add salt and pepper to taste, then pour into a warm serving dish, and serve immediately.

Serves 8

Per serving: Calories: 48, Protein: 1 gm., Fat: 0 gm., Carbohydrates: 11 gm.

Steamed Ohio Pudding
with Brandy Sauce

This is an old-fashioned, American steamed pudding which contains not only no suet, but no fat of any kind! And yet it's moist and delicious due to the grated raw carrot and potato.

If you have a pressure cooker, you can steam the pudding without the pressure valve for 20 minutes, then at 10 lbs. pressure for 60 minutes. Let the pressure drop naturally.

The pudding can be made several days ahead of time, then reheated by steaming for about 30 minutes.

Lightly oil a 2-quart bowl or pudding mold. Heat water in a pot large enough to hold the mold.

In a large bowl, mix the sugar, flour, baking powder, salt, soda, and spices. Add the dried fruit and grated vegetables, and mix everything together very thoroughly with your hands. Press the mixture into the mold, and cover with the lid, oiled brown paper, or a double layer of foil, tied in place with string.

Place the mold on a rack in the pot of water, so that the water comes halfway up the side of the mold. Cover and steam for 3 hours, keeping at a simmer and adding boiling water when the water level goes down.

Remove the pudding from the water, and cool on a rack for 10 minutes before unmolding it onto a serving platter. Serve warm with brandy sauce.

To make the brandy sauce, mix together the water, sugar, cornstarch, and salt in a small saucepan. Bring to a boil, stirring, over high heat. When it thickens, allow it to boil for 1 minute. Remove from the heat and stir in the brandy or brandy flavoring.

Serves 8

1 c. sugar or Sucanat
1 c. whole wheat pastry flour
2 tsp. baking powder
1 tsp. salt
1 tsp. baking soda
½ tsp. ground cinnamon
½ tsp. ground ginger
½ tsp. ground allspice

1 c. raisins (or other dried fruit, chopped)
1 c. currants (or other dried fruit, chopped)
1 c. raw potato, peeled and finely grated
1 c. raw carrot, peeled and finely grated

Brandy Sauce
1 c. water
½ c. Sucanat or brown sugar
3 T. brandy (or use 1 tsp. brandy flavoring)
1 T. cornstarch
pinch of salt

Per serving: Calories: 314, Protein: 3 gm., Fat: 0 gm., Carbohydrates: 71 gm.

Mocha Bûche de Noël
Yule Log Cake

The original of this luscious Christmas cake "log," a sponge cake roll with rum and a mocha-flavored, butter cream icing, is France's most famous holiday specialty.

The popularity of this cake in many European countries reflects the importance of the burning of the Yule log in ancient times. The power of the Yule log, particularly birch, gave its strength to the newborn sun at the beginning of a new solar year.

Our version uses the fat-free Basic Holiday Cake Roll and is iced with a glossy, coffee-flavored, chocolate icing. Decorate the "log" with holly.

Basic Holiday Cake Roll, plain, chocolate, or almond variation (pgs. 154-55)
Sweet "Cream Cheese" Filling (p. 154), but use strong, brewed coffee instead of the water and rum instead of the lemon juice

Lean Mocha Frosting
½ c. reduced-fat soymilk
½ c. strong, brewed coffee or coffee substitute
¾ c. sugar or Sucanat
⅔ c. unsweetened cocoa
⅓ c. cornstarch

1 tsp. pure vanilla extract

Follow the directions on pages 154-55 for making the cake roll and the filling, and for filling and rolling the cake.

To make the frosting, mix the soymilk, coffee, sugar, cocoa, and cornstarch in a blender until it is very smooth. Pour this into a heavy, medium saucepan, and stir constantly over medium heat with a wooden spoon, scraping the bottom and sides often. Cook for about 7 minutes, or until the mixture is thick and glossy.

Remove the pan from the heat, and add the vanilla. Beat the mixture with a wire whisk to remove any lumps. Cool the mixture completely, stirring occasionally.

If you make it ahead of time, refrigerate it but bring to room temperature before frosting the cake, and beat it again to make it smooth. If the mixture is too thick, whip in a little maple syrup until it is the right consistency.

To decorate the cake, cut the ends off the cake at a slant, and save the pieces to use as "knots." Place the roll on a serving platter, and ice the cake roll all over with the cooled frosting. Ice the "knots" too, and attach them to the cake where you like. Use a knife to make swirls in the icing.

Serves 8 to 10

Per serving: Calories: 302, Protein: 8 gm., Fat: 2 gm., Carbohydrates: 62 gm.

Afro-Brazilian-Caribbean Kwanzaa Karamu or Feast

Although Kwanzaa started 30 years ago in the United States, it is only in the last few years that I've noticed articles about Kwanzaa festivities and food in "mainstream" magazines. Kwanzaa is a non-political, non-denominational, African-American cultural holiday which was the dream of Dr. Maulana (Ron) Karenga, a leading theorist of the Black Movement. Kwanzaa means "first fruits of the harvest" in the East African language of Kiswahili. Since 1966, the spirit of Kwanzaa has grown continually, and now over 5 million North Americans celebrate Kwanzaa instead of, or in addition to, Christmas.

Dr. Karenga borrowed from many African harvest festivals to create this unique holiday, which is a time to focus on Africa and African-inspired culture. It is non-religious, but definitely spiritual, and has a structure which allows for personal interpretation and offers a great opportunity for creativity. Individual families create their own Kwanzaa traditions. Some people use African-inspired ornaments to "Kwanzaafy" their Christmas tree and other Christmas decor. In some communities, there may be public dance performances, readings, exhibits, and the like with African themes during Kwanzaa week.

On each of the seven days of Kwanzaa, the focus is on one of the Seven Fundamental Principles of Kwanzaa (called *Nguzo Saba*): unity (*umoja*); self-determination (*kujichagulia*); collective work and responsibility (*ujima*); cooperative economics (*ujamaa*); purpose (*nia*); creativity (*kuumba*); and faith (*imani*).

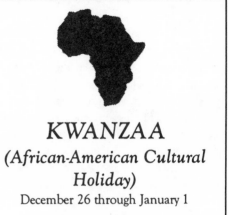

KWANZAA
(African-American Cultural Holiday)
December 26 through January 1

MENU

Vegetarian Jamaican "Patties"
(savory stuffed pastries)

Vegetarian Feijoada
(black beans and rice)

Kwanzaa Greens

Louisiana hot sauce

sliced peeled oranges

Melon and Cucumber Salsa

Mashed Sweet Potatoes and Pineapple

Baked yams
(white-fleshed)

ginger beer, lemonade, or fruit punch

Lemon Pie

A table is set aside to display the symbols of Kwanzaa: *mazao* (fruits and vegetables, which signify the product of unified effort); *mkeka* (an African place mat of straw or cloth that represents reverence for tradition); *vibunzi* (an ear of corn, or one ear for each child); *zawadi* (simple gifts, preferably handmade, or related to education or African culture); *kikombe cha umoja* (the Unity Cup or communal cup for libations); *kinara* (the seven-branched candelabra, which symbolizes the continent and peoples of Africa); and *mishumaa saba* (the seven candles, each one symbolizing one of the Nguzo Saba or Seven Fundamental Principles—one black candle for the people; three red for the struggles of the people, and three green for the Motherland, Africa)

On each day of Kwanzaa, a family member lights a candle for one of the Seven Principles, using the middle black candle to light it and alternating from the green candles on the left to the red candles on the right. Those present are asked to think of the ways they can use the Nguzo Saba in their daily lives.

On the evening of December 31, a feast called the Kwanzaa Karamu is held. This is usually a potluck and encompasses a wide variety of foods. The table (or floor) should be decorated in African motifs with black, green, and red colors, and a large *mkeka* (place mat). Guests are encouraged to dress in African-influenced clothing, hairstyles, jewelry, head wraps, etc.

Besides welcoming statements, African and African-inspired music, dance, poetry, storytelling, drumming, chanting, singing, and readings, a libation (usually water, as the essence of life) is poured from the Unity Cup in the Four Directions, and then passed around for everyone to sip from. The *tamshi la tambiko* or libation statement is recited (see the bibliography on page 185 for books that contain more information on this).

The names of family ancestors and black heroes are called, and the feasting commences! The feast should be a fusion of modern American, native African, and all of the other influences of black culture—West Indian, Brazilian, and Creole. Since the African diet is primarily one of grains, vegetables, and fruits, a vegetarian feast is appropriate, and many creative, vegetarian African-American cooks are replacing the smoked meats of "soul food" dishes with vegetarian broths, liquid smoke, hot spices, and roasted sesame seeds.

Our Afro-Brazilian-Caribbean Kwanzaa Karamu features one of my favorite company dishes, a vegetarian feijoada from Brazil—spicy black beans with rice, cooked greens, and sliced oranges. Not only is it one of the most delicious and nutritious meals, but it is so simple to make in quantity, and the colors are absolutely stunning.

This menu could also be used as an exotic harvest, Thanksgiving, Labor Day, wedding, or birthday feast.

Vegetarian Jamaican "Patties"
Savory Stuffed Pastries

*S*picy stuffed pastries with a rich, curried pastry crust are sold by street vendors all over Jamaica. Phyllo pastry brushed with curry broth makes a crispy, fat-free stand-in for the pastry, and a spicy textured vegetable protein filling is irresistible.

To make the filling, steam-fry the onions, jalapeños, and garlic in a large, heavy, nonstick or lightly oiled skillet until the onion is limp. Add the tomato and green onions. Steam-fry until most of the liquid has evaporated. Add the 2 teaspoons curry powder, salt, thyme, and allspice, and stir-fry for a minute. Add the reconstituted textured vegetable protein and the lemon juice or sherry, mix well, and allow to cool.

Heat the vegetarian broth with 1 teaspoon curry powder until dissolved. Set aside to cool completely.

To fill the "patties," stack 3 sheets of phyllo together, and cut into four 6" x 5" rectangles. Repeat with the remaining phyllo. Keep the phyllo well-covered with plastic wrap while you work.

For each "patty," place about 3 tablespoon of the filling in one corner of a rectangle of phyllo. Roll the filled end toward the center, then fold in the left and right corners like an envelope, then roll up again. (See illustration, p. 61.) Cover the filled "patties" with plastic wrap while you fill the rest.

Preheat the oven to 400°F. Place the filled "patties," seam side down, on nonstick or lightly oiled cookie sheets. Brush or spray the tops lightly with the cooled curry broth. Bake the "patties" for about 20 minutes, or until golden

Filling
2 large onions, minced
2 T. chopped pickled jalapeño peppers
    (or Scotch bonnet peppers)
2 cloves garlic, minced

1 large tomato, chopped
½ c. green onions, minced

2 tsp. curry powder
1 tsp. salt
½ tsp. dried thyme
¼ tsp. ground allspice

1½ c. dry textured vegetable protein
    granules, reconstituted in 1 cup +
    2 T. boiling water with 2 T. soy sauce
2 T. lemon juice or dry sherry

1 c. vegetarian broth
1 tsp. curry powder

9 full sheets phyllo pastry

brown. Serve hot. (These can be made ahead and reheated.)

Makes 36 to 48 "patties"

Per patty: Calories: 26, Protein: 2 gm., Fat: 0 gm., Carbohydrates: 5 gm.

Vegetarian Feijoada

U se a large platter or tray to serve this dish—mound the rice around the edge of the dish, and fill the center with the beans, using a pitcher for the bean broth. Serve with Kwanzaa Greens, sliced, peeled oranges, sliced onions which have been marinated in vinegar for several hours, Louisiana hot sauce, and salsa, vinegar, or lemon juice.

Beans
4 c. dried black (turtle) beans
12 c. vegetarian broth
4 medium onions, chopped
1 (28 oz.) can diced tomatoes and juice
4 large cloves garlic, minced
2 tsp. dried oregano
1 tsp. liquid smoke
½ tsp. cayenne pepper

Rice
4 c. long-grain brown or brown basmati
  rice
6 c. water
1 tsp. salt

8 oranges, peeled and sliced ¼" thick

Place the dried beans (unsoaked) in a large pot with the broth and other ingredients (except rice). Bring to a boil, boil for several minutes, then reduce heat, cover, and simmer for 2 to 3 hours, or until beans are tender. Taste for salt.

To pressure-cook, you need a large, canning-sized pressure cooker, or you can do it in two batches in a 6-quart pressure cooker. Cook the bean ingredients at 15 lbs. pressure for 40 minutes.

About an hour before serving, heat a large, heavy saucepan with a tight lid. Add the dry rice and stir it over high heat with a wooden spoon for 2 minutes. Slowly add the water and then the salt. Bring to a boil, cover, and reduce heat to low. Simmer for 45 minutes. Remove from the heat and let stand about 15 minutes before serving.

Mound the drained beans in the center of a large serving platter, and surround them with the rice. Arrange the orange slices attractively on a separate plate, and pass the bean broth in a pitcher.

Serves 8 to 10

Per serving: Calories: 605, Protein: 23 gm., Fat: 2 gm., Carbohydrates: 123 gm.

Kwanzaa Greens

Collard greens are the preferred green, leafy vegetable for cooking in the American South and in West Africa, but in some northern areas, they are hard to find unless you grow them yourself. (One cup of cooked collards contains 357 grams of calcium, among other things, so like the other greens mentioned here, this easy-to-grow vegetable is worth planting in your garden.) You can use your favorite green, or a mixture of collards, turnip greens (my favorite), kale, mustard greens, or spinach.

The traditional, Southern way to cook greens is with smoked pork. Here we use vegetarian broth, liquid smoke, lots of onions, and garlic, for plenty of flavor without the fat. Soy bacon chips or vegetarian "back bacon" or "ham," chopped up, can be sprinkled on top, if you like. Red bell pepper mixes with the greens to reflect the colors of Kwanzaa too.

The large amount of broth used results in a nutritious "pot liquor" which is eaten with the greens in bowls. Even though the greens are cooked for quite a long time compared to the way we usually cook greens, nothing is lost when the "pot liquor" is enjoyed along with the greens.

If you say you don't like greens, this recipe may change your mind for good!

Fill your kitchen sink with lukewarm water, and add the greens, trimmed of roots, tough stems, and yellowed leaves—if using spinach, wash it separately. (This looks like a lot of greens, but they cook down a lot.) Swish the greens around to remove grit. Lift the greens out, leaving the grit in the water, and drain well in a colander.

Repeat this procedure as many times as necessary to remove any dirt, depending upon the size of your sink.

In a large, lightly oiled, heavy-bottomed pot, steam-fry the onion and garlic until limp. Add the broth and bring to a boil. Add the greens in batches, filling the pot and then cooking at high heat until they go limp enough to push down into the broth. Add another batch and repeat until all the greens are used up. (If using some spinach, don't add it at this point—spinach cooks much more quickly than other greens.) Sprinkle with liquid smoke.

(cont.)

4-5 lbs. fresh greens (collard greens, turnip greens, mustard greens, kale, or spinach, or a mixture)

2 large onions, minced
6 cloves garlic, chopped

6 c. vegetarian broth
a few shakes of liquid smoke

2 large red bell peppers, seeded and diced

salt and freshly ground black pepper to taste
Louisiana hot sauce and vinegar on the side
soy bacon chips or chopped vegetarian "back bacon" or "ham" to sprinkle on top (optional)
Sesame Meal (p. 175) to sprinkle on top (optional)

Cover and cook at a simmer for 45-60 minutes, or until the greens are tender, adding spinach and peppers when only 20 minutes of cooking time is left. Taste for salt and pepper. Serve the hot greens and "pot liquor" in bowls with vinegar and hot sauce, and the optional Sesame Meal, soy bacon chips, and/or chopped vegetarian "ham" or "back bacon" on the side.

Serves 8 to 10

Per serving: Calories: 63, Protein: 3 gm., Fat: 0 gm., Carbohydrates: 11 gm.

Melon and Cucumber Salsa

T his "salsa" is a bit like an Indian raita or salad—a cool but spicy mixture of fruit, vegetables, herbs, and spices. It's great with the feijoada. Melons are available just about everywhere any time of the year, but substitute more tropical fruits, such as mango or papaya, if you can get ripe, tasty ones.

about 1 lb. of cucumber, peeled
4 c. ripe cantaloupe or other favorite melon, diced
1 medium red or sweet onion, chopped
¼ c. fresh lime juice
¼ c. cilantro, chopped
1 T. pickled jalapeño pepper, minced
1 T. honey or alternate liquid sweetener
½ tsp. salt

chile powder to sprinkle on top

Dice the cucumber and mix in a serving bowl with all of the ingredients except the chile powder. Cover and refrigerate until serving time (up to 4 hours). Before serving, stir well and sprinkle the top lightly with chile powder.

Serves 8

Per serving: Calories: 71, Protein: 1 gm., Fat: 0 gm., Carbohydrates: 15 gm.

◆◆

Mashed Sweet Potatoes
and Pineapple

This recipe began as one using mashed winter squash, but it is delicious with mashed sweet potatoes too. The tropical flavors of pineapple and ginger go well with this exotic menu.

To cook the sweet potatoes, you can use one of several methods:

1) Scrub the sweet potatoes, prick them all over, and bake at 400°F for 40-50 minutes, or until soft.

2) Peel sweet potatoes and cut into 1½" chunks, place them in a large, shallow baking pan with a bit of hot water in it, cover, and bake at 400°F for 20-30 minutes, or until soft.

3) Peel sweet potatoes and cut into 1" cubes; steam them for 15 minutes, or until soft.

4) Cut the sweet potatoes in half, cover, and boil in water for about 20 minutes, or until soft.

Whichever way you cook them, scoop the flesh out of the peels if cooked whole; drain if cooked in chunks. Mash the soft sweet potato with a potato masher. Whip in a bit of the reserved pineapple juice to make it the consistency you like. Beat in the ginger and salt to taste. Spread the mashed sweet potato into a shallow, lightly oiled casserole. Spread the crushed pineapple or pineapple tidbits over the top. This can be made ahead and baked before serving.

Preheat the oven to 350°F. Bake the casserole for 40-50 minutes.

Serves 8 to 10

Per serving: Calories: 247, Protein: 2 gm., Fat: 0 gm., Carbohydrates: 59 gm.

---

12 medium sweet potatoes (orange)

1 (19 oz.) can crushed pineapple or pineapple tidbits in unsweetened pineapple juice, drained (reserve juice)
1 tsp. ground ginger
salt to taste

Lemon Pie

This delicious, creamy pie is so easy to make that I'm sure it will become a favorite all year round.

1 (9") No-Fat Vanilla Cookie Crumb
Crust, pre-baked for 5 minutes
(p. 162)

Filling

1 lb. reduced-fat, medium-firm, regular
tofu
¾ c. white or turbinado sugar,
or ½ c. light honey
½ c. lemon juice (preferably fresh, but
bottled will do)
2 T. cornstarch
grated zest of 1 large lemon,
or 2 tsp. lemon extract

Optional "Meringue" Topping

1⅓ tsp. agar powder (or 2 T. + 2 tsp.
agar flakes) mixed with ¼ c. cold
water
¾ c. cold water
½ c. powdered egg replacer
½ c. white or turbinado sugar
4 tsp. pure vanilla extract
½ tsp. pure lemon extract

Preheat the oven to 350°F.

Combine the filling ingredients together in a blender or food processor until very smooth. Pour this into the crust, and bake for 35 minutes. Cool the pie on a rack, then refrigerate.

To make the optional "meringue," mix the agar and water in a small saucepan, and let sit for about 5 minutes. Stir over medium heat until it simmers, then allow to simmer 1 minute.

In a deep, medium bowl, beat the egg replacer and ¾ cup water with an electric or rotary egg beater until like softly mounded egg whites. Beat in the sugar, vanilla, and lemon extract, then the cooked agar mixture. Beat well to distribute the agar evenly. When smooth and glossy, cool it in the refrigerator. It will firm up. Beat it again briefly, then pile the mixture around the edge of the pie, leaving the edge of the crust and the center showing. Make little peaks in the "meringue" with the back of a spoon. Refrigerate until ready to serve.

Serves 8

Per serving: Calories: 210, Protein: 8 gm., Fat: 3 gm., Carbohydrates: 40 gm.

Greek New Year's Eve Dinner

New Year's Eve is a night of revelry in many cultures. We stay up late to welcome the New Year with loud noisemaking, parties, and toasting. This is true in Greece as well as here in North America, but with a difference. January 1st is also St. Basil's Day, St. Basil being one of the fathers of the Greek Orthodox Church.

At home, there is much feasting, visiting, and merriment. Children put their shoes in front of the fireplace before they go to bed for St. Basil to fill with gifts. The grown-ups play cards or other gambling games until midnight (to see what their luck will be in the New Year!), when the children are awakened to join in the toasts and greetings, and to open their gifts, of course!

Housewives have been baking for days, making pastries, sweets, and savory Basil cakes. Nuts, tangerines, oranges, and pomegranates are kept on the table during the holidays. Before the champagne toast, the Vasilópita, or St. Basil's Bread, is brought in by the women, who are dressed in their finest clothes and jewelry.

The lights are dimmed and everyone hugs, kisses, and greets one another with "Hronia polla!" or "Many happy years!" The lights are turned back on, and the Sign of the Cross is made over the bread before the first cut is made by the head of the household. Great good luck goes to the person who finds a coin hidden in

NEW YEAR'S EVE
December 31

MENU
Spanikopita Rolls

Dolmathes

sliced tomatoes, red onions, bell peppers, and cucumbers
sprinkled with red wine vinegar, salt, and pepper

Spanakórizo

Moussaka
or Pastisio

Crusty Bread
(purchased or homemade, p. 149-50)

Vasilópita (p.147)

tangerines, oranges, and pomegranates

Greek coffee or espresso

champagne, sparkling fruit juice,
or non-alcoholic sparkling wine

No-Bake Tofu Cheesecake Pie
with Apricot Topping

his/her piece, a custom which dates back to the heyday of Byzantium. At last the champagne is poured (if it can be afforded), toasts are made, and the gambling goes on until dawn.

I can't think of any better New Year's Eve feast than a delicious Greek meal! I think you'll love our vegan versions of Spanikopita (spinach pie) and Moussaka (eggplant casserole) or Pastisio (Greek macaroni casserole).

Spanikopita Rolls
Little Greek Spinach-Phyllo Pies

The filling for these little pies is a bit unusual, containing such un-Greek ingredients as tofu, nutritional yeast, and miso! But these unconventional ingredients give the filling a rich, feta-like taste, which is what you expect from spanikopita. (I took these to a potluck once, and they were gobbled up before the hostess even got to taste one—no one even suspected that they were dairy-free!) If you use frozen, chopped spinach, the filling takes only minutes to make and can be made ahead (although you should make the rolls shortly before serving).

Filling
1½ lbs. reduced-fat, medium-firm,
    regular tofu, drained and crumbled
¼ c. light miso
2 T. nutritional yeast flakes
1 tsp. salt

3 (10 oz.) pkgs. frozen chopped
    spinach, thawed and squeezed dry,
    or 3 lbs. fresh spinach, cleaned,
    steamed, squeezed dry and
    chopped (you can substitute nettles,
    chard or other greens for all or part
    of the spinach)
1 bunch green onions, chopped and
    steam-fried until soft
2 T. dried dillweed (or ½ c. fresh,
    chopped)

12 full sheets of phyllo pastry, thawed
    and kept covered

soymilk for brushing tops

Per roll: Calories: 38, Protein: 3 gm., Fat: 1 gm., Carbohydrates: 5 gm.

Prepare the filling (you can do this a day or two ahead of time) by mixing the tofu, miso, yeast, and salt together very well in a large bowl. Use your hands, a potato masher, or a fork. Add the squeezed-dry, cooked or frozen spinach, the steam-fried green onions, the dill, and mix well.

To fill the rolls, stack three sheets of phyllo together, and cut the stack into four 6" x 5" rectangles with a pair of kitchen scissors or a sharp knife. Repeat with the remaining phyllo. You should have 48 rectangles. Keep the phyllo well-covered with plastic wrap while you work. Preheat the oven to 400°F.

For each spanikopita, place about 3 tablespoons of filling in one corner of a rectangle of phyllo. Roll the filled corner toward the center, then fold in the left and right corners, like an envelope, then roll up again (see illustration for *Samosas*, p. 37). Cover the filled spanikopita with plastic wrap while you finish.

Place the filled rolls, seam side down, on nonstick or lightly oiled, dark cookie sheets. Brush the tops with soymilk. Bake for 20 minutes, or until golden brown. Serve hot.

Makes about 48 rolls

Dolmathes
Grape Leaves Stuffed with Rice

S tuffed grape leaves are as beloved in Greece and the Middle East as stuffed cabbage leaves in Slavic countries, with as many variations! Although Greek restaurants in North America usually feature them with a meat stuffing, a rice stuffing is also traditional.

Look for jars of grape leaves in brine in delicatessens, Middle Eastern or Greek markets, or large supermarkets. If you have a grape arbor, you can pick tender grape leaves in June and use them fresh (just blanched for a minute), or blanch them and freeze them for later use. Don't substitute brown rice in these—the acid in the lemon juice used in the recipe hardens the bran covering and makes it difficult for the rice to cook to a soft state. These should be served at room temperature, so they can be made ahead of time.

Prepare the grape leaves by carefully separating them and rinsing them under cold running water as you work. Pour boiling water over them, then drain and rinse again. Place any broken or torn ones, or very small ones, on the bottom of a heavy cooking pot. You should have 36 usable leaves.

To make the filling, steam-fry the minced onions and green onions in a lightly oiled or nonstick frying pan until soft and transparent. Add the rice, parsley, dill, salt, pepper, 1 cup of water, and raisins, if using. Cover and simmer about 10 minutes, or until the liquid is absorbed—the rice will be undercooked, but will cook further later.

To fill the leaves, place a heaping teaspoon of filling in the center of each grape leaf. (If any stems remain, snip them off with scissors, and discard.) Fold up the stem end, then fold the

12 oz. jar of grape leaves (you need 36 usable leaves)

Filling
2 large onions, minced
6 green onions, minced

1 c. raw basmati or converted (par-boiled) rice
1 c. fresh parsley, minced
1 tsp. dried dillweed
1 tsp. salt
¼ tsp. black pepper
¼ c. raisins (optional)

Cooking Broth
1¼ c. lightly-salted vegetarian broth
¼ c. lemon juice

sides over the filling. Roll the leaf up firmly, but not too tightly (the filling will expand somewhat). Place seam side down in the leaf-lined pot. Continue, layering tight rows of little rolls.

Mix together the lemon juice and broth, and pour this over the rolls. Place an inverted dinner plate over them, to keep them weighted down a little and prevent them from opening up. Cover,

Tofu Mint Sauce
½ (10.5 oz.) pkg. reduced-fat, firm,
    SILKEN tofu, or 4 oz. reduced-
    fat, firm, regular tofu
¼ c. lemon juice
½ tsp. dried mint, crumbled (or 1 T.
    fresh)
¼ tsp. salt
pinch of sugar or alternate sweetener

Garnishes
lemon wedges
fresh parsley and/or mint sprigs

bring to a boil, then turn down low and simmer for 1 hour.

Carefully remove the rolls from the pot (using tongs, if possible), place them on a serving plate, and garnish with the lemon wedges and greens. Allow to cool.

Make the Tofu Mint Sauce by mixing the sauce ingredients (add 2 tablespoons water if using regular tofu) until *very* smooth in a blender or food processor. Refrigerate the sauce until serving time, and serve with the dolmathes.

Makes about 36 dolmathes

Per dolmatha: Calories: 22, Protein: 1 gm., Fat: 0 gm., Carbohydrates: 4 gm.

Moussaka
Eggplant Casserole
& Pastisio (Greek Macaroni Casserole)

Moussaka is one of the first ways that North Americans become acquainted with eggplant, usually in a Greek restaurant. Unfortunately, although the dish is scrumptious, it is full of fatty meat and olive oil, and topped with a rich, savory custard sauce made with egg yolks.

Our version is still delicious, but the eggplant is broiled instead of fried in olive oil (eggplant soaks up oil like a sponge!); textured vegetable protein supplies the bulk in a savory tomato sauce flavored with wine, mushrooms, cinnamon, and oregano; and a creamy, light sauce based on potatoes tops the casserole. To make this dish easier on the cook, divide the steps up, and make the sauces on one day, then cook the eggplant and assemble and cook it on the next day.

For those who dislike eggplant, we provide an alternative version, the Greek baked macaroni casserole, pastisio, which basically substitutes layers of cooked macaroni for the eggplant. (Kids tend to prefer this version.)

Prepare the Tangy Cream Sauce, and set aside. Place the eggplant slices on a nonstick or lightly oiled cookie sheet, and broil them (in batches) about 4" from the heat until slightly charred on each side and soft in the middle. Set aside.

To make the tomato sauce, steam-fry the onions and garlic in a large, nonstick or lightly oiled pot, until beginning to soften and brown. Add the mushrooms and steam-fry until the liquid evaporates. Add the remaining sauce ingredients, including the reconstituted textured vegetable protein, and simmer for about 20 minutes. Add a bit of water if it's too thick (but it should be thicker than spaghetti sauce). Add salt and pepper to taste. (If you want a "meatier" taste, use soy sauce instead of salt.)

1 recipe Tangy Cream Sauce (p. 73)
4 large eggplants (peel if desired), thinly
    sliced

Tomato Sauce
5 large onions, minced
6 large cloves garlic, minced
1 lb. fresh mushrooms, chopped
2 c. dry textured vegetable protein
    granules, soaked in 1⅔ c. boiling
    water and ¼ c. soy sauce
2 (6 oz.) cans tomato paste
2 c. water
⅔ c. dry red wine
¼ c. fresh parsley, chopped
1 T. dried oregano
2 tsp. dried basil or rosemary
½ tsp. freshly ground black pepper
¼ tsp. ground cinnamon
small bay leaf
salt and black pepper to taste
freshly grated nutmeg

(cont.)

Preheat the oven to 375°F.

To assemble the casserole, in a nonstick or lightly oiled, 9" x 13" casserole or baking pan, spread one-third of the tomato sauce. Layer half of the eggplant slices over this, then another third of the tomato sauce, then the remaining eggplant. Spread the last third of tomato sauce over the eggplant. Dribble the Tangy Cream Sauce over the top, and spread it evenly. Sprinkle it lightly with nutmeg.

Bake the casserole for 45 minutes, and let stand for 15 minutes before cutting into 8 servings.

Serves 8

Per serving: Calories: 287, Protein: 17 gm., Fat: 1 gm., Carbohydrates: 46 gm.

---

3 (10 oz.) packages frozen chopped spinach
2 large onions, minced
4 c. tomato juice (you can use the juice from canned tomatoes)
1½ c. basmati or converted (parboiled) rice
2 tsp. salt
½ tsp. freshly ground black pepper
½ tsp. dried dillweed or mint

soy parmesan or crumbled Tofu Feta (p. 175—optional garnish)

---

ings. Stir briefly, bring to a boil, then cover and turn down to low. Cook for 35 minutes. Remove from heat and keep covered until serving time.

Serves 8

Pastisio

(Greek Macaroni Casserole)

Omit the eggplant and cook 1 lb. of dry elbow macaroni in plenty of boiling salted water until tender, but not soft. Drain the macaroni.

Make a double recipe of the Tangy Cream Sauce. Mix half of it with the macaroni, and save the other half for the topping. Preheat the oven to 350°F.

In a nonstick or lightly oiled, deep 9" x 13" (or larger) casserole or baking pan, spread half the macaroni, then half of the tomato sauce, then the other half of the macaroni, then the last half of the tomato sauce. Spread the remaining Tangy Cream Sauce over the top, and sprinkle lightly with nutmeg. Bake 45 minutes, then let the casserole stand for 15 minutes before cutting into 8 servings.

Per serving: Calories: 319, Protein: 20 gm., Fat: 3 gm., Carbohydrates: 48 gm.

Spanakórizo
Spinach and Rice Pilaf

This dish may be a common one in Greece, but it is uncommonly delicious! It can make a great main dish for an everyday meal too.

Thaw and drain the spinach, but do not squeeze it dry. In a large, nonstick or lightly oiled saucepan, steam-fry the onion until it is soft. Add the spinach, tomato juice, rice, and season-

Per serving: Calories: 167, Protein: 5 gm., Fat: 0 gm., Carbohydrates: 35 gm.

No-Bake Cheesecake Pie
with Apricot Topping

This is not a Greek dessert, but a combination of a creamy, cheese-like filling and an apricot topping that reminds me of the Greek "spoon sweets," or fruit preserves that are eaten with a spoon. It makes a great ending for this festive meal.

The day before, start the topping by soaking the chopped apricots in apple juice to cover overnight. The next day, simmer the apricots and juice, uncovered, over low heat, stirring frequently, until the apricots are very soft and the liquid is absorbed. Remove from the heat and add the honey, lemon juice, water, and extract. Pour into a bowl, cover with plastic wrap, and cool.

To make the crust, either microwave on HIGH for 2 minutes, or bake at 350°F for 5 minutes; then cool while you make the filling.

To make the filling, mix the water and agar in a small saucepan, let it sit for a few minutes, then stir constantly over high heat until it boils. Turn it down and simmer gently for 3 minutes. Add the crumbled tofu to the pot along with the sugar and lemon juice. Stir until the tofu is hot to the touch (this is important so that the agar does not gel too quickly). Pour this into a blender or food processor with the extracts and salt, and blend until very smooth, stopping and scraping the mixture down a couple of times. Pour the mixture into the prepared pie pan, and smooth the top. Refrigerate until firm and cold, at least 2 hours.

Spread the apricot mixture evenly over the top before serving. Cut into 8 wedges.

Serves 8

Apricot Topping
1 c. dried apricots, chopped
apple juice to cover
2 T. honey or liquid fruit juice concentrate
1 T. lemon juice
1 T. water
2 drops of pure almond or lemon extract

1 (9") No-Fat Vanilla Cookie or Graham Cracker Crumb Crust (p. 162)

Cheesecake Filling
¾ c. plus 2 T. water
½-¾ tsp. agar powder or 1-1½ T. agar flakes (use the greater amount for a firmer filling)

1½ (10.5 oz.) pkgs. reduced-fat, extra-firm, SILKEN tofu, crumbled
⅓ c. sugar (turbinado is fine)
2 T. lemon juice

1 tsp. pure lemon extract
½ tsp. pure vanilla extract
½ tsp. coconut extract (optional)
¼ tsp. salt

Per serving: Calories: 219, Protein: 7 gm., Fat: 2 gm., Carbohydrates: 42 gm.

Holiday Baking and Desserts

One of the most challenging aspects of no-added-fat cooking is making delicious baked goods and desserts. There is no point in making desserts—which are treats, after all (or should be!) —that are dry, tasteless, and unappealing. I have come to the conclusion that if there is some special bread or dessert that means a lot to your family for special occasions, and you can't revise it to lower the fat and still taste good, go ahead and serve it once in a while—but serve one or two of these almost-no-fat options as well. Give yourself, your family, and guests a choice.

Low-Fat Baking Tips

Crusty yeast breads are easily made with no fat. Soft yeast breads can be made nearly fat-free by using soymilk, mashed potatoes, and an acid ingredient, such as lemon juice, to tenderize the gluten. Make the dough as moist as possible, but otherwise treat it the same as any yeast bread.

Quick breads and cakes made without added fat are best when made with pastry (low-gluten) flour, and/or the addition of another flour, such as oat flour. In most recipes, the fat tenderizes the gluten. In a fat-free bread, it's better just to start with less gluten, or the results will be tough and dry. Stir batters as briefly as possible.

To some extent, corn syrup and honey, applesauce, or prune and other fruit purees can take the place of fat in quick breads and sweet baked goods, but I find that whipping tofu with the sugar and liquid usually results in a lighter, more moist product that doesn't dry out quickly.

Soymilk or tofu can also take the place of eggs in many recipes, but powdered egg replacer can be whipped with cold water, using a electric or rotary beater, until it is like softly-mounded egg whites. This can add lightness and structure to some recipes. (Use 1½ tsp. powdered egg replacer mixed with 2 tablespoons water for 1 egg; or 2 tsp. powdered egg replacer beaten with 2 tablespoons of water for 1 egg white.)

A little bit of nutritional yeast or soy flour can sometimes be added to make up for the rich flavor of egg yolks that might be missing. (Lecithin, by the way, contains 14 grams of fat per tablespoon, so is not a good substitute for egg yolks in low-fat cooking.)

If the recipe calls for nuts, seeds, or coconut, you can omit it or substitute chopped, dried fruit or no-oil granola (and sometimes dry-roasted soybeans or chickpeas). Add a tiny bit of almond, coconut, or other nut extract for flavor. Coconut extract, especially, seems to add richness to many recipes.

Unsweetened cocoa powder (or carob, if you prefer) is used in this book instead of chocolate because virtually all of the fat has been removed.

Dairy products and eggs have natural sodium, so it is necessary to add a bit of salt to these recipes to make up for this. Other ways of adding flavor to fat-, egg-, and dairy-free baking and desserts are to use a little more vanilla, other extracts such as pure lemon and orange, brandies and flavored liqueurs, citrus zests, spices and herbs, or fruit juices for the liquid.

When a recipe you are converting calls for skim milk, use reduced-fat soy or other non-dairy milk; for evaporated milk, use full-strength soy milk; for buttermilk, use soymilk curdled with a bit of lemon juice or vinegar; for ¼ cup of instant skim milk powder, use 2 tablespoons of soymilk powder or other non-dairy milk powder. Reduced-fat, medium-firm, regular tofu mashed with a bit of soymilk can substitute for ricotta cheese; mixed with Tofu Sour Cream it can replace cottage cheese.

A note on paper liners: Paper liners stick to non-fat mixtures, so don't use them. Use non-stick muffin tins, or lightly oiled or sprayed tins. Cool cupcakes or muffins on a rack covered with a clean tea towel to soften the crust (which tends to be a little tough even if the inside is moist and tender). The outside of non-fat muffins or cakes is often chewier than the full-fat versions, but softens by the next day.

Powdered Turbinado Sugar
or Powdered, Granulated Sugar Cane Juice (Sucanat®)

G ranulated sugar cane juice is available under various brand names, like Sucanat, in most natural food stores. It is unrefined and tastes like a light brown sugar; some brands use organic sugar cane.

Place the ingredients in a *dry* blender, and blend at high speed until the sugar is powdery. You may have to stop the machine from time to time and shake the mixture. Store in an airtight container.

Makes 1 cup

Per Tbsp.: Calories: 47, Protein: 0 gm., Fat: 0 gm., Carbohydrates: 11 gm.

---

1 c. turbinado sugar or granulated sugar cane juice (Sucanat)
1 T. cornstarch (or other starch)

Starch Glaze

This simple glaze is used in place of egg white to help toppings adhere to the tops of loaves or for a shiny crust.

½ c. cold water
1 tsp. cornstarch

Mix the water and cornstarch together in a small saucepan. Stir constantly over high heat until thickened and clear.

Makes ½ cup

Per Tbsp.: Calories: 1, Protein: 0 gm., Fat: 0 gm., Carbohydrates: 0 gm.

Sweet Glaze

This is brushed onto breads after they've been baked and are still hot for a sweet, shiny glaze.

Heat equal parts of *reduced-fat soymilk* and *honey or other syrup* together in a small saucepan over medium heat. *Do not boil* or it will curdle.

Per Tbsp.: Calories: 35, Protein: 0 gm., Fat: 0 gm., Carbohydrates: 8 gm.

◇◇◇

Powdered Sugar Glaze

W hite cane sugar is always bleached with beef bone ash (beet sugar is not), so if you are a vegetarian and you aren't sure what kind of sugar is available, you may prefer to use turbinado sugar, a light, beige sugar which is steam-cleaned; or granulated sugar cane juice. You can powder it yourself in a blender (see Powdered Turbinado Sugar, p.141).

In a bowl or food processor, mix together the ingredients to make a thick, smooth, spreadable icing. For a thin glaze, spread it on hot cake or bread. For a thicker glaze, spread it on after the cake or bread has cooled.

Makes enough for 1 cake or loaf

Per Tbsp.: Calories: 29, Protein: 0 gm., Fat: 0 gm., Carbohydrates: 7 gm.

> 1 c. powdered sugar (icing or confec-
> tioner's sugar),
> or Powdered Turbinado Sugar,
> or Powdered Granulated Sugar Cane
> Juice (p. 141)
> ½ tsp. pure vanilla or other flavor
> extract
> 1½ T. soymilk (you can use juice for
> different flavor)

White Glaze

T his is a good alternative for anyone who doesn't want to or can't use sugar, even in the form of granulated sugar cane juice. Don't use a cheap, bulk soymilk powder for this recipe—you must use a low-fat, vegan "milk" powder which tastes good as a cold beverage.

Mix the ingredients together thoroughly in a small bowl or a food processor. If you want a thin glaze, spread it on hot bread or cake. For a thicker glaze, spread it after the bread or cake has cooled.

Makes enough for 1 loaf or cake

Per Tbsp.: Calories: 43, Protein: 3 gm., Fat: 0 gm., Carbohydrates: 7 gm.

> ½ c. powdered, high-quality soymilk or
> light tofu beverage mix,
> or other good-tasting, low-fat, vegan
> "milk" powder
> 2-4 T. honey or alternate liquid
> sweetener
> ¼ tsp. pure vanilla or other flavor
> extract

◇◇

Yeast Breads and Variations

Fat-Free
Sweet Yeast Bread Dough

T his is a great, basic dough for breads that usually call for eggs and butter–it's light and moist and just slightly sweet. I'll give you a few variations to make special holiday breads, but please experiment by adapting your own favorite sweet breads to this dough.

To make hamburgers buns, soft savory breads, or rolls, omit the sugar and honey, or use only 2 tablespooons honey. Use only ½ a packet or 1½ tsp. of yeast. Omit the wheat germ and add 1 cup whole wheat flour. Turmeric is optional. You can add herbs to this or use it for filled breads like calzone.

2 c. warm water
1 pkg. or 1 T. regular baking yeast

1 c. leftover mashed potatoes (½ lb.
    russet potatoes, cooked and
    mashed),
    or 1 c. instant mashed potato flakes
    mixed with ⅔ c. boiling water
½ c. wheat germ
¼ c. soymilk powder
¼ c. honey
¼ c. sugar
1 T. lemon juice
2 tsp. salt
¼ tsp. turmeric

5 c. unbleached all-purpose flour

In a large mixing bowl or the bowl of a heavy-duty mixer, combine the water and yeast. When the yeast has dissolved, add the mashed potatoes, wheat germ, soymilk powder, honey, sugar, lemon juice, salt, and turmeric. Mix in the unbleached flour. Knead well for 5-10 minutes (using as little flour as possible if kneading by hand—the dough should be soft and a bit sticky).

Place the dough in an oiled bowl which will allow for doubling of the dough. Turn it over to oil the top, and cover with plastic wrap, or place inside of a large plastic bag (to prevent the dough from drying out). Rise overnight or for 8-12 hours in the refrigerator (this dough handles best when cold).

Several hours before serving, shape the dough into two loaves, 16 large rolls, or 32 small rolls, according to the recipe variation you are using. Cover and let rise in a warm place until doubled. Bake at 350°F for 20-45 minutes, depending upon the size and shape of the loaves or rolls. (Solid round or pan loaves may take as long as 45 minutes; long, braided, or ring loaves about 30 minutes; small rolls 20 minutes.) Cool on racks and decorate as directed in the variation recipe.

Makes 2 loaves or 32 small rolls

Per small roll: Calories: 91, Protein: 3 gm., Fat: 0 gm., Carbohydrates: 18 gm.

Challah

Jewish Sabbath Bread

Divide the risen *Sweet Yeast Bread Dough* equally in half. Shape into two braided loaves. Just before baking, brush with Starch Glaze (p. 142), and sprinkle with *sesame or poppy seeds.* Bake as for loaves in the basic recipe.

Makes 2 loaves

Sprial Challah

with Raisins

Add *1 cup golden or sultana raisins* to the *Sweet Yeast Bread Dough.* Divide the risen dough in half, and roll each half on a floured surface to make about a 30"-long "rope." On a nonstick or lightly oiled baking sheet, form each rope into a spiral, tucking the end of the rope underneath. Bake as directed, brushing the loaves with *soymilk* before placing in the oven.

Makes 2 loaves

Il Bollo

Italian-Jewish Yom Kippur Bread

Add to the *Sweet Yeast Bread Dough: 2 T. whole anise seeds, 2 tsp. vanilla,* and *1 tsp.* of *grated lemon zest or lemon extract.* Shape the risen dough into 2 oval loaves about 12" long, and place on nonstick or lightly oiled baking sheets. Brush the tops with *soymilk* before baking. Bake as directed.

Makes 2 loaves

Three Kings' Cake
Rosca de Los Reyes

This traditional Mexican sweet bread is usually served on Twelfth Night (Epiphany), but it can be served anytime during the holiday season. It makes a great breakfast bread.

Traditionally, an unshelled almond, a ring, or a coin is rolled up in each loaf with the fruit. Whoever gets this prize is assured good luck in the coming year. If you do this, warn your guests so that they don't inadvertently bite into it and crack a tooth!

1 recipe Fat-Free Sweet Yeast Bread
  Dough (p. 144-45)
1 tsp. ground anise seeds
2 c. mixed glacéed fruit, chopped,
  or mixed dried fruits, chopped (if
  they are very dry, soften slightly by
  soaking briefly in hot water)
Double recipe for Powdered Sugar
  Glaze (p. 143),
  or double recipe for White Glaze
  (p. 143), flavored with pure lemon
  extract instead of vanilla
additional glacéed or chopped dried
  fruit for decorating

Makes 2 loaves

Per slice: Calories: 153, Protein: 3 gm., Fat: 0 gm., Carbohydrates: 34 gm.

The evening before serving, follow the directions for the Fat-Free Sweet Yeast Bread Dough, adding the ground anise seed along with the turmeric.

The next morning, remove the risen dough from the refrigerator, and divide it exactly in half. Lightly flour your work surface, and keep the second half of the dough covered while you work with the first. Roll each half of the dough into a rectangle about 8" wide and 24" long. Sprinkle each half with 1 cup of the fruit. Roll each rectangle lengthwise jelly-roll fashion, and pinch the edge of the dough to the body of the roll to seal.

Place each roll seam side down on a lightly oiled cookie sheet, and shape into a ring. Press the ends together to seal. Cover and let rise in a warm place until puffy, about 1 to 1½ hours.

Preheat the oven to 350°F. Bake the rings until golden, about 30 minutes. Transfer loaves carefully to wire racks, and cool. Decorate with one of the glazes and the additional fruit (the fruit is meant to look like jewels in a crown).

Vasilópita
St. Basil's Bread or Greek New Year's Bread

V asilópita is traditionally baked with a gold or silver coin in it, and the person who gets this slice is said to have good luck in the year to come. If the slice cut for St. Basil or the Holy Mother has the coin in it, the coin is donated to the poor at the local church. After each guest is handed a slice, he or she searches for the coin; if none is found, he/she says, "No coin." Everyone yells, "Poor loser!" The finder is loudly cheered for good fortune.

The Greek spice mahlepi–originally from Persia–comes from the hard, small seed of a flowering tree similar to a cherry. You can find it in Greek and Middle Eastern grocery stores, but if you are unable to locate it, you can make a liquid substitute. Simmer together over low heat for 20 minutes: 3 whole cloves, ½ stick of cinnamon, 1 bay leaf, and ¾ cup water. Strain and use 2 tablespoons for every 1 tablespoon of mahlepi called for. (From Cooking and Baking the Greek Way by Anne Theoharous, Holt, Rinehart and Winston, New York, 1977.)

To the *Fat-Free Sweet Yeast Bread Dough*, add 2 tsp. *pure almond extract* and 1 T. of *ground mahlepi* (a Greek spice) or 2 T. of *mahlepi substitute* (see above). Make the risen dough into 2 round loaves. When the loaves have risen, brush them with *Starch Glaze* (p. 142), and make a decoration on the top (the number of the New Year, or a simple flower pattern) with *sliced almonds*. Brush the breads with glaze again, and sprinkle with *sesame seeds*. Bake as directed.

Makes 2 loaves

Panettone

I always make this Italian sweet bread at Christmas–it makes great toast!

To the *Fat-Free Sweet Yeast Bread Dough*, add 2 tsp. *pure almond extract*, 1 T. *anise seed* (crushed or ground, if possible), 1 cup *candied fruitcake mix* or chopped, *mixed dried fruits*, and ½ cup *raisins*. Form the risen dough into 3 round loaves. Cut a cross ½"-deep across the top of each loaf, using a razor blade or sharp knife. Rise until doubled. Brush the tops of the loaves with *soymilk* before baking as directed in the Yeast Bread recipe. You can serve Panettone plain or iced with *Powdered Sugar Glaze* (p. 143) or *White Glaze* (p. 143) and sprinkled with colored candy sprinkles.

Makes 3 loaves

◆◆◆

Italian Easter Bread

*T*his bread is usually made with colored eggs baked into it, but they can be omitted, if you like.

Make the same dough variation as for *Panettone*, p. 147. Cut the risen dough in half. Form each half into two 24"-long "ropes." Twist two ropes together loosely, and form a ring on a nonstick or lightly oiled baking sheet. Repeat with the remaining two ropes. Rise and bake as directed in the Yeast Bread recipe. Ice the cool bread with *Powdered Sugar Glaze* (p. 143) or *White Glaze* (p. 143), and sprinkle with *colored candy sprinkles*.

Makes 2 loaves

Hot Cross Buns

*T*hese little, spicy buns are traditional in English-speaking countries on Good Friday, but they originated before Christianity.

To the *Fat-Free Sweet Yeast Bread Dough*, add 1 cup dried currants or raisins, ²/₃ cup candied fruitcake mix or chopped, mixed dried fruit, 1½ tsp. vanilla, 1½ tsp. cinnamon, ½ tsp. nutmeg, and ¼ tsp. EACH *ground ginger and allspice*. Form the risen dough into 32 balls, and place them in two nonstick or lightly oiled 9" x 13" baking pans, leaving a little space between the rolls. Let rise until doubled. Cut crosses in the tops of the buns with a razor blade just before baking as directed in the Yeast Bread recipe. After baking, brush the hot buns with *Sweet Glaze* (p. 142). Make crosses on the tops of the buns with a thick *Powdered Sugar Glaze* (p. 143) or *White Glaze* (p. 143), flavored with a few drops of *pure almond extract*.

Makes 32 buns

Basic French, Italian, or Crusty Bread
and Hard Rolls

I n some areas you can buy delicious, crusty breads fresh from a bakery, but there is nothing like fresh, crusty breads from your own oven. This type of bread is actually a very simple one and easy to make. Just remember not to try and speed it up—it needs time to develop flavor and texture. It also needs a hot oven and some moisture at the beginning of the baking, to develop "oven spring" (the last burst of rising) and to form a golden crust.

You will notice that this bread contains no sweetener or oil. The yeast can feed off the natural sugars in the flour, so it needs no sugar. The lack of oil gives the bread a crisp crust and chewy texture (as you would expect with this type of bread), but makes it stale fast. If you aren't going to eat it within a day, freeze it.

NOTE: You can make this dough in a large food processor or in two batches in a medium food processor, processing for about 30 seconds. Omit the first rising of the "sponge."

In a large bowl or bowl of a heavy-duty mixer, dissolve the yeast in the water for about 5 minutes. Stir in the first 3 cups of flour and the salt. Beat well, cover with plastic wrap, and let this "sponge" (batter) rise for 1 or 2 hours in a warm spot or overnight in the refrigerator.

Stir in the last 3 cups of flour a little at a time, adding only as much as necessary to make a kneadable dough. Knead the dough with the dough hook of a heavy-duty mixer or by hand on a lightly floured surface for about 10 minutes. Add a little more flour as needed, but be careful not to make the dough too dry—it should be moist, but not sticky, and very pliable.

Slam the dough down hard on your work surface a few times after kneading (to get rid of

1 T. regular baking yeast
2 c. very warm water
3 c. unbleached or whole wheat flour
2 tsp. salt
3 c. unbleached all-purpose flour
Starch Glaze (p. 142)

◇◇

air bubbles). Place the dough in a large, lightly oiled bowl, cover well, and let rise at room temperature until doubled. Punch down. If you like, let it rise once again, but this isn't necessary.

Punch the dough down and divide it in half. Shape the dough into 2 long loaves, rounds, or braided loaves, or into 12-16 loaf-shaped rolls. Place on nonstick or lightly oiled cookie sheets sprinkled with cornmeal or semolina cereal. Sprinkle the tops with flour, cover, and let rise at room temperature until doubled.

Meanwhile, preheat the oven to 425°F.

In order to generate steam in the oven, you can place a shallow pan of hot water in the bottom of the oven, or squirt the loaves and the walls of the oven two or three times in the first 10-15 minutes of baking with cold water in a plant mister.

Before baking, slash the loaves in several places with a razor blade. If using the spray method for humidity, spray the loaves before putting them in the oven, and every 5 minutes for two times after they start to bake. If you are using a pan of water in the oven, remove it after the first 15 minutes of baking. Brush the loaves with Starch Glaze, and bake 15-20 minutes more, or until the bread is a rich, golden brown. (Rolls will take less time.) Remove the bread from the pans, and cool on racks.

When the bread has cooled, you can freeze it wrapped in foil, then reheat it wrapped in the foil at 350°F for 20 minutes (or in the microwave wrapped in a paper towel for 1-2 minutes).

Makes 2 loaves or 12 to 16 rolls

Per roll: Calories: 173, Protein: 6 gm., Fat: 0 gm., Carbohydrates: 36 gm.

◇◇◇

Foccaccia

We used to buy tomato foccaccia (pronounced foh-káh-cha) by the slice in Italian grocery stores in San Francisco, where I grew up, but the foccaccia from Genoa, where my paternal grandmother came from, is more often an herb and olive oil version. I make it both ways now, but I use my Roasting and Grilling Marinade instead of olive oil, with great success.

Foccaccia makes a great snack, open-face sandwich bread, or accompaniment to soup or salad.

Preheat the oven to 450°F. Roll half the risen *Basic Italian Bread* dough (p. 149-50) to fit an 11" x 15" cookie sheet (nonstick or lightly oiled). Don't make a rim, as you would for pizza. Make deep dents in the dough at intervals with your fingertips. Spread the dough *thinly* with *tomato sauce* (or you can use *crushed tomatoes, chopped fresh tomatoes, or even the juice from canned tomatoes*) or *Roasting and Grilling Marinade* (p. 178). For a stronger flavor, you can use *Balsamic Dressing* (p. 68) instead of the marinade. Sprinkle the dough with *lots of fresh basil, oregano, rosemary, or other favorite herbs* (or a smaller amount of dried herbs). Now you can either bake it or add more toppings, such as a sprinkling of soy parmesan; freshly ground black pepper, red chile flakes, or minced hot peppers; roasted garlic, chopped garlic, or garlic granules; steam-fried onion and/or bell peppers; grilled eggplant slices; soaked or marinated dried tomatoes (not the oil-packed variety); *Low-fat Pesto* (p. 95) or *Dried Tomato and Mushroom Tappenade* (p. 93); or whatever else appeals to you.

Bake (without rising) for 12-15 minutes, or until the bottom is golden and crispy, and the edges are browned. Cut into 2" x 5" strips while hot. Can be frozen.

Makes two 11" x 15" foccaccias

Cakes and Cupcakes

Making cakes without butter, shortening, oil, eggs, or dairy products is quite a challenge! Making ones that are moist and light seems almost a contradiction in terms. However, I have come up with a basic formula based on the *Light and Easy Cake* recipes used in my first cookbook, *The Almost No-Fat Cookbook*, but with the addition of beaten, powdered egg replacer and water to give it more structure. This formulation (half the recipe) is used in the rolled cake recipes in the Valentine's Day, Easter, and Christmas menus.

I've also included a delicious, fat-free fruitcake which I've used for many years, based on the old, boiled-raisin cake recipe of the '30s and '40s.

Basic
Almost Fat-Free Bundt Cake
or Cupcakes

T his is the cake recipe to use for birthday cakes and possibly even wedding cakes (perhaps in conjoined tube or bundt cake circles, like "wedding rings," or stacked tube cakes of progressively smaller sizes). To keep the outside of the cake moist, either cool it covered with a clean tea towel, or apply a hot, sweet glaze to the crust before cooling. The crust softens and the texture of the cake improves after a day in the refrigerator, well-wrapped with plastic wrap after cooling.

Liquid Ingredients
1 lb. reduced-fat, medium-firm, regular tofu,
  or 2 (10.5 oz.) pkgs. reduced-fat, firm, SILKEN tofu
2 c. sugar, Sucanat, or alternate sweetener
2 T. lemon juice or vinegar
2 T. water
2 T. pure vanilla or citrus fruit extract or liqueur of choice,
  or use 1 T. pure vanilla extract and ½ tsp. pure almond extract

---

Preheat the oven to 350°F.

Mix the liquid ingredients in a food processor or blender until smooth. Whisk together the dry ingredients in a medium bowl. In a small, deep bowl, beat the cold water and egg replacer with an electric or rotary beater until it is like softly mounded, beaten egg whites.

Pour the liquid ingredients into the dry ingredients, and mix as briefly but smoothly as possible. Fold in the beaten egg replacer with a rubber spatula, distributing it thoroughly but gently. Spoon the batter evenly into a 10" nonstick bundt or tube pan sprayed lightly with nonstick spray, or 18 nonstick, lightly oiled or sprayed muffin cups.

Bake in the center of the oven for 45 minutes for the cake, or 25 minutes for cupcakes. Test the center with a cake tester or toothpick. Let cool in the pan 5 minutes, then loosen carefully and invert on a rack. Cover with a tea towel, and glaze with *Sweet Glaze* (p. 142) either while still warm or after cooling thoroughly. Alternately, after cooling, you can frost it with *Powdered Sugar Glaze* (p. 143), *White Glaze* (p. 143), *Lean Mocha Frosting* (p. 124), or other favorite icing. Refrigerate until the icing is firm, then wrap in plastic wrap, and refrigerate until the next day. Slice carefully with a sharp serrated knife.

Makes 1 (10") tube or bundt cake
or 18 cupcakes

Per serving: Calories: 163, Protein: 5 gm., Fat: 1 gm., Carbohydrates: 34 gm.

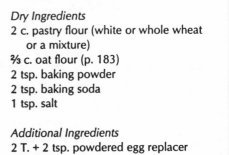

Dry Ingredients
2 c. pastry flour (white or whole wheat
  or a mixture)
⅔ c. oat flour (p. 183)
2 tsp. baking powder
2 tsp. baking soda
1 tsp. salt

Additional Ingredients
2 T. + 2 tsp. powdered egg replacer
1/2 c. cold water

Lekakh

Jewish Honey Cake

Omit the sugar, extract, lemon juice or vinegar, and 2 T. water from the liquid ingredients. In place of these ingredients, use *1 cup Sucanat, brown sugar, or alternate, and ¾ cup honey (or fruit syrup concentrate).* Add to the dry ingredients *½ cup chopped, pitted dates* and *½ cup raisins.* Optional spices are: *1 tsp. ground cinnamon, 1 tsp. ground nutmeg,* and *½ tsp. ground cloves.* Use *½ cup strong brewed coffee or coffee substitute* instead of the additional water beaten with the powdered egg replacer.

Chocolate Cake

Omit the oat flour and use *⅓ cup unsweetened cocoa powder* instead. Use *vanilla extract or a coffee or chocolate liqueur,* and use vinegar instead of lemon juice.

◇◇◇

Basic Holiday Cake Roll

Thıs could also be used for a jelly roll. Be sure to use pastry flour for a tender cake.

Cake Batter
8 oz. reduced-fat, medium-firm, regular tofu,
   or 1 (10.5 oz.) pkg. reduced-fat, firm, SILKEN tofu
1 c. sugar or Sucanat
1 T. lemon juice
1 T. water
2 tsp. pure vanilla extract

1 c. unbleached white pastry flour
⅓ c. oat flour (p. 183)
1 tsp. baking soda
1 tsp. baking powder
¾ tsp. salt

¼ c. cold water beaten with 4 tsp. powdered egg replacer

Sweet "Cream Cheese" Filling
1 T. cold water
1 T. lemon juice
½ tsp. agar powder (or 1 T. flakes)

¼ c. honey or alternate liquid sweetener
1 (10.5 oz.) pkg. reduced-fat, extra-firm, SILKEN tofu, crumbled
½ tsp. pure vanilla extract,
   or ¼ tsp. pure almond or coconut extract

To make the cake, preheat the oven to 350°F. In a blender or food processor, mix the tofu, sugar, water, lemon juice, and vanilla until very smooth.

In a medium bowl, whisk together the flours, baking soda, baking powder, and salt.

In a small bowl, beat the powdered egg replacer and the water with a hand-held electric mixer until it is like softly mounded egg whites.

Pour the blended mixture into the flour mixture, and stir together briefly but thoroughly. Fold the beaten egg replacer mixture into the batter with a rubber spatula, thoroughly but gently, just as you would beaten egg whites.

To make a roll, scrape the batter onto a 10" x 15" jelly roll pan, lightly oiled and lined with waxed paper, also lightly oiled. Smooth the batter very evenly, and bake for 10 minutes. Have a clean tea towel ready, sprinkled generously with powdered sugar (or unsweetened cocoa powder for a chocolate roll). As soon as you take the cake from the oven, loosen the sides and carefully invert the cake on the powdered tea towel. Carefully remove the waxed paper. Sprinkle the cake with more powdered sugar (or cocoa powder). Fold one end of the tea towel over one short end of the cake, and carefully start rolling the cake AND the towel into a jelly roll shape, trying not to crack it. (You must do this while the cake is hot.) Set the rolled cake aside to cool thoroughly before filling.

To make the "cream cheese" filling, mix the water, lemon juice, and agar in a small saucepan, and let soak for 5 minutes. Bring to a boil over high heat, stirring. Stir in the honey and add the tofu. Stir over high heat until the tofu is hot (this is important so that the agar doesn't gel too fast). Pour into a blender or food processor with the vanilla, almond, or coconut extract. Blend until very smooth. Chill in a bowl until the mixture is spreadable, but not completely cold.

To fill the roll, carefully unroll the cake. Spread the entire cake with the filling, as evenly as possible.

Then, using the tea towel as a guide but keeping it out of the way, roll the cake up again, as neatly as possible. Set it seam-side-down on a serving plate, cover with plastic wrap, and refrigerate until serving time.

If appropriate, ice and decorate the cake roll according to the directions for the specific holiday cake roll you are making. Carefully cut the roll into slices with a serrated knife, using a gentle sawing motion.

Makes 8 to 10 servings

Per serving: Calories: 194, Protein: 7 gm., Fat: 1 gm., Carbohydrates: 40 gm.

Chocolate Cake Roll

Increase the vanilla to 1 tablespoon, and substitute ⅓ *cup unsweetened cocoa* for the oat flour.

Almond Cake Roll

Add 1 *teaspoon pure almond extract* along with the vanilla to the cake ingredients.

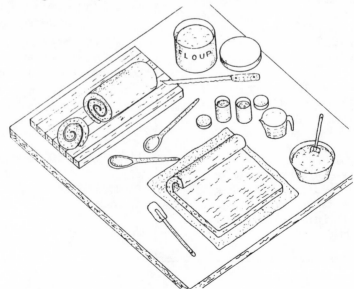

Carrot Fruitcake

This is a dark fruitcake, which I prefer. You can make a light fruitcake by omitting the spices and using all light sugar or more honey (or alternate) instead of molasses, unbleached flour rather than whole wheat, and golden raisins, dried pineapple, and candied cherries for the fruit. Another variation would be to omit 1/3 cup of the flour and add 6 tablespoons unsweetened cocoa powder.

You can wrap the cooled loaves in liquor-soaked cheesecloth and keep them for several weeks, or simply wrap in foil (in which case they should be frozen after about 1½-2 weeks).

Bring the boiled mixture ingredients to a boil together in a medium saucepan, then reduce heat and simmer for 10 minutes. Set aside to cool.

Preheat the oven to 300°F.

In a large bowl, mix together the dry ingredients, then add the cooled boiled mixture and the dried fruits. Mix well and spoon into two 3" x 6" loaf pans (fruitcake pans) and one 8" x 4" loaf pan, nonstick, lightly oiled, or sprayed and lined on the bottom with waxed paper or cooking parchment. Bake the small loaves for 45 minutes and the larger loaf for 60 minutes. Invert on racks to cool. Carefully peel off the paper.

Makes two 3" x 6" loaves plus one 8" x 4" loaf

Per slice: Calories: 196, Protein: 2 gm., Fat: 0 gm., Carbohydrates: 45 gm.

Boiled Mixture
1½ c. water or apple juice (can
    substitute ½ c. with liquor of choice)
1 c. carrots, grated
1 c. raisins
1 c. sugar or alternate sweetener,
    or ½ c. honey plus ¼ c. molasses
¼ c. applesauce
1 tsp. ground cinnamon
1 tsp. salt
¼ tsp. ground cloves

Dry Ingredients
1½ c. whole wheat flour
½ c. oat flour (p. 177)
1 tsp. baking soda

Dried Fruits
2 c. mixed, dried fruits, whole or
    chopped (or candied fruitcake
    mix, if you prefer)
1 c. pitted dates, whole or chopped
1 c. dried currants

◇◇

Cookies, Bars, and Squares

It's difficult to make a cookie that is crispy or moist when you use no fat, but I have worked out a few excellent recipes that I don't hesitate to serve to company. These may not replace your traditional holiday cookies, but they'll enable you to offer your guests and family a tempting choice.

Almost No-Fat Brownies

I f you prefer, you can make these delicious morsels with carob powder instead of cocoa. For a rich treat, spread the bars with a thin layer of Lean Mocha Frosting (p. 124).

Preheat the oven to 350°F. In a blender or food processor, mix the sugar, tofu, cocoa, water, egg replacer, coffee granules, vanilla, and vinegar until smooth.

In a medium bowl, whisk together the flour, salt, baking powder, and soda. Add the cocoa mixture and mix briefly.

Pour the mixture into a nonstick, lightly oiled, or sprayed 7" x 11" or 8" x 8" cake pan, and spread evenly. Bake 25 minutes. Cool on a rack in the pan, then cut into 16 bars.

Makes 16 bars

Per brownie: Calories: 72, Protein: 2 gm., Fat: 0 gm., Carbohydrates: 14 gm.

---

1 c. Sucanat or sugar
4 oz. reduced-fat, medium-firm, regular tofu
½ c. unsweetened cocoa or carob powder
¼ c. water
4 tsp. powdered egg replacer
1 T. coffee or coffee substitute granules
2-3 tsp. pure vanilla extract or liqueur
1½ tsp. vinegar

⅓ c. unbleached flour
½ tsp. salt
½ tsp. baking powder
½ tsp. baking soda

◆◇◆

Basic Fat-Free
Cookie Dough

This dough makes a cookie that is crispy-chewy on the outside and a bit cakey—but not dry—on the inside. It's great!

NOTE: Since these are rolled in sugar to make a crispy crust and keep the insides moist, these cookies can easily burn. If you don't have the new, double-bottomed cookie sheets, line your sheets with baking parchment or oiled brown paper.

Blended Ingredients
8 oz. reduced-fat, medium-firm, regular tofu
½ c. corn syrup (or you can use a rice or fruit concentrate syrup)
1½ c. sugar or alternate sweetener
1 T. pure vanilla extract or other extract

Dry Ingredients
3 c. pastry flour (white or whole wheat)
1 c. oat flour (p. 183), brown rice flour, or other low-gluten flour
1 tsp. salt
1 tsp. baking powder
1 tsp. baking soda

Additional Ingredients
½ c. cold water mixed with 2 T. plus 2 tsp. powdered egg replacer

For rolling the cookies
½ c. sugar, Sucanat, or cinnamon-sugar

Preheat the oven to 350°F.

Combine the blended ingredients in a blender or food processor until smooth. Whisk the dry ingredients together in a medium bowl. In a medium bowl, beat the water and egg replacer with an electric or rotary beater until like softly mounded beaten egg whites. Add the tofu mixture to the egg replacer mixture, and stir well. Add this to the flour mixture, and mix thoroughly.

Drop rounded teaspoons of the dough into the ½ cup sugar, and shape them into balls with your hands. Place the balls on the prepared cookie sheets (see above)—you will need four, or do two batches of two pans each. Place the balls well apart, and do not press down. Bake in the top half of the oven for 12 minutes. Cool the cookies on racks. If not eaten the same day, they should be frozen.

Makes 56 cookies

Per cookie: Calories: 59, Protein: 1 gm., Fat: 0 gm., Carbohydrates: 13 gm.

Fudge Chews

Instead of the oat flour, use *1 cup unsweetened cocoa powder*. Use pure vanilla extract.

Ginger Crinkles

Use *½ cup dark molasses* instead of corn syrup. Omit vanilla or other extract. Add *1 T. powdered ginger, 1 tsp. cinnamon*, and *½ tsp. ground cloves*. You could also add some chopped candied ginger, if you wish.

Jam Thumbprints

Use white flour and a light sugar. Use *2 tsp. vanilla* and *1 tsp. coconut extract*. After the cookies are baked, make a thumbprint indentation in each one, and fill each with *¼ tsp. thick jam, jelly marmalade*, or *lemon curd (you'll need about 5 T. in all)*.

Chinese Chewies

T hese bars (and I have no idea where they got the name!) have been a favorite Christmas cookie of ours for years. The original recipe contained eggs and chopped walnuts, but these are delicious too.

Preheat the oven to 350°F.

In a medium bowl, whisk together the flour, baking powder, and salt. In a small, deep bowl, beat together the water and egg replacer with an electric or rotary beater until like softly mounded, beaten egg whites. Mix in the sugar and beat until almost stiff. Scoop this into the bowl with the flour mixture, along with the dates and granola. Mix gently but well.

Scoop the mixture into a nonstick, lightly oiled, or sprayed 8"-square cake pan. Bake for 25 minutes, or until it begins to turn golden (it will be soft). Cool slightly on a rack, then cut into small pieces and roll in powdered sugar. Cool thoroughly and store in an airtight container.

Makes about 32 squares

¾ c. whole wheat pastry flour
1 tsp. baking powder
¼ tsp. salt

4 tsp. powdered egg replacer mixed
    with ¼ c. cold water

1 c. Sucanat, brown sugar, or alternate
    sweetener
1 c. pitted dates, chopped
1 c. No-Oil Granola (p. 179)
powdered sugar or Powdered Turbina-
    do Sugar (p. 141)

Per piece: Calories: 63, Protein: 1 gm., Fat: 0 gm., Carbohydrates: 14 gm.

Biscotti

These fat-free, twice-baked Italian cookies are delicious dunked in coffee, tea, or hot cocoa. We especially love the chocolate version.

½ c. cold water mixed with 2 T. plus 2 tsp. powdered egg replacer

1 c. Sucanat or sugar
2 tsp. pure vanilla, lemon or orange extract (or 1 tsp. pure almond or other nut extract)

2 c. pastry flour (white or whole wheat)
1 tsp. baking powder
½ tsp. baking soda
½ tsp. salt
1 c. dried apricots, cherries, raisins, currants, or other dried fruit, chopped, or 3 T. candied ginger, minced (optional)

Preheat the oven to 325°F. In a medium bowl, whisk or beat the water and egg replacer together until frothy. Mix in the sugar and extract, and beat well.

In another bowl, whisk together the flour, baking powder, soda, and salt. Stir this into the egg replacer-sugar mixture, along with the optional fruit. Mix well and, with floured hands, shape the dough into two 3"-wide "logs," nine to ten inches long, with ends squared off. Place these on a nonstick, lightly oiled, or sprayed cookie sheet. Bake the "logs" for 25 minutes. Remove the pan and reduce the oven heat to 300°F.

Cool the "logs" on a rack for 15 minutes. Cut the "logs" carefully with a serrated knife straight across into 14 slices each. Place the slices cut side down on two nonstick, lightly oiled, or sprayed cookie sheets. Bake 10-12 minutes. Turn the slices over and cook 10-15 minutes more. Cool on racks, then store airtight for up to two weeks.

Makes 28 biscotti

Per cookie: Calories: 54, Protein: 1 gm., Fat: 0 gm., Carbohydrates: 12 gm.

Chocolate

Instead of 2 cups pastry flour, use 1 cup pastry flour and *1 cup unsweetened cocoa.* If you wish, add *1 tsp. of instant coffee* to the water mixed with the egg replacer.

Mocha

Omit ¼ cup of the flour and use ¼ cup *unsweetened cocoa powder.* Use ½ *cup of cold, strong brewed coffee or espresso* instead of water to beat with the egg replacer. Use *1 tsp. pure almond extract* as the flavoring.

Anise

Use *1 tsp. pure almond extract* for the flavoring, and add *2 tsp. ground anise seeds.*

Pies and Tarts

You can make some surprisingly rich-tasting and delicious pies and tarts with very little fat. Several recipes are sprinkled throughout the book, but here I give you a few more and three pie crust recipes—two with no fat at all. One has about half the fat of ordinary pastry, a higher-fat option for those recipes which you or your family may feel are just not the same for special occasions with a no-fat crust.

Low-Fat Oil Pastry

*A*lthough this crust does contain fat, it has about half that of ordinary pastry, and it uses oil rather than hard fat. Divided into 8 servings, each piece with either a bottom or a top crust (not both) and a fat-free filling will contain 5 grams of fat. The pastry flour and soured soymilk make a tender crust that no one will guess is low-fat!

This recipe first appeared in the November 1994 issue of Vegetarian Times.

Mix the flours in a medium bowl with the salt, baking powder, and sugar. Whisk together the soured soymilk and oil in a cup until well blended. Pour this into the flour mixture, and mix gently with a fork until it holds together in a ball. If it's too dry, sprinkle with a tiny bit of water. If you have time, place the dough in a plastic bag, and refrigerate it for an hour before rolling out. Roll out and bake as you would an ordinary crust.

For savory pies, you can add ½ tsp. curry powder, if you like.

Makes one 9" crust

½ c. unbleached all-purpose flour
½ c. MINUS 1 T. whole wheat pastry flour
⅜ tsp. salt
⅜ tsp. baking powder
⅜ tsp. sugar or Sucanat

3 T. soymilk with ½ tsp. lemon juice added
3 T. oil (I use canola)

Per serving: Calories: 94, Protein: 2 gm., Fat: 5 gm., Carbohydrates: 10 gm.

◇◇◇

No-Fat
Cookie or Graham Cracker Crumb Crust

Now that there are commercial cookies and graham crackers made without fat (check your health food store), we can make delicious crumb crusts that are more tender than those made with cereal. One caution, though—these crusts tend to get soggy the day after baking if they are filled, so plan to serve them the same day, or bake but don't fill them the day before serving.

1½ c. fat-free, vanilla cookie or fat-free graham cracker crumbs
3 T. maple or alternate syrup
¼ tsp. coconut extract or pure almond extract (optional)

Mix the ingredients together well, and press onto the bottom and sides of a nonstick, lightly oiled, or sprayed 9" pie pan, leaving no holes. Bake at 350°F for 5 minutes, or microwave on HIGH for 2 minutes, then fill and bake as directed, or cool thoroughly before filling with a no-bake filling.

Makes one 9" crust

Per serving: Calories: 123, Protein: 2 gm., Fat: 0 gm., Carbohydrates: 28gm.

Chocolate Crumb Crust

Use *fat-free, chocolate cookie crumbs* in the *Cookie Crumb Crust* instead of vanilla or graham cracker cookie crumbs, or add *1 T. unsweetened cocoa powder* to the basic crust.

Yeasted Pastry Dough

I t's impossible to make a flaky pastry without fat, but I really like this tender, yeasted pastry for cooked fruit pies and quiches. You can make a conventional, double crust pie, but I prefer to make a "freeform" pie. This is rolled into one large circle with the edges folded up over the filling and baked free-standing on a cookie sheet rather than a pie pan (see illustration, p. 83). It makes a lovely, home-style dessert.

Mix the warm soymilk, mashed potatoes, honey, and baking yeast in a medium bowl or food processor; let stand for 5 minutes.

Add the unbleached flour and salt. Knead for 5 minutes or process in the food processor for 30 seconds.

Place the dough in an oiled bowl, cover with plastic, and let rise in a warm place until doubled (30-60 minutes) or in the refrigerator for up to 24 hours. If refrigerating, oil the top of the dough lightly, and cover well with plastic to prevent drying out.

To make a double crust pie, preheat the oven to 350°F, divide the dough in half, and roll one half to fit the bottom of a lightly oiled, 9" pie plate. Fill the pie with your favorite filling, and cover with the second half of the dough, rolled to fit the top. Crimp the edges together, and cut slits in the top for steam to escape. Bake immediately for 25-30 minutes or until golden. The pie may be glazed before baking with soymilk and a sprinkling of sugar, or after baking with maple syrup or apple juice concentrate.

To make a "freeform" pie, preheat the oven to 350°F, roll the dough out on a floured surface into a 16" circle, and place it carefully on a lightly oiled cookie sheet or pizza pan. Make sure there are no holes or excessively thin spots in the dough. Pile the filling in the center, and drape

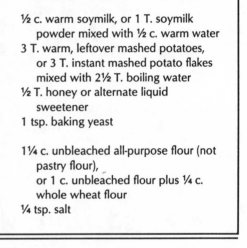

½ c. warm soymilk, or 1 T. soymilk
    powder mixed with ½ c. warm water
3 T. warm, leftover mashed potatoes,
    or 3 T. instant mashed potato flakes
    mixed with 2½ T. boiling water
½ T. honey or alternate liquid
    sweetener
1 tsp. baking yeast

1¼ c. unbleached all-purpose flour (not
    pastry flour),
    or 1 c. unbleached flour plus ¼ c.
    whole wheat flour
¼ tsp. salt

the edges up over the filling, "pleating" it attractively and leaving about a 5" hole in the center (see illustration, p. 83). Bake immediately for about 25-30 minutes or until golden, glazing it either before or after baking as for 9" pie above.

Makes a double 9" crust or a 10" freeform pie

Per serving: Calories: 75, Protein: 2 gm., Fat: 0 gm., Carbohydrates: 15 gm.

◆◇◆◇◆◇◆◇◆◇◆◇◆◇◆◇◆◇◆◇◆◇◆◇◆◇◆◇◆◇◆◇◆◇◆◇◆◇◆

"Buttertarts"

Buttertarts are a Canadian tradition, especially at Christmas. Usually made with a rich pastry and an egg-y, buttery filling, these delicious little treats are made with the Low-Fat Oil Pastry and the fat-free Maple Syrup-Granola Tart filling from p. 108, at less than 4 grams of fat per tart!

1 recipe Low-fat Oil Pastry (p. 161)
1 recipe Maple Syrup-Granola Tart
   Filling* (p. 108), using 1 tsp. vanilla
   and ⅔ c. raisins instead of the
   granola (or ⅓ c. raisins and ⅓ c.
   granola)
1 T. rum added to the filling (optional)

*If you prefer, you can use dark corn
   syrup instead of the maple syrup.

Make the Maple Syrup-Granola Tart Filling with the suggested changes, stirring in the raisins after cooking. Preheat the oven to 450°F.

Roll out the pastry on a lightly floured board, and cut into 12 four-inch circles. Fit the circles gently into 12 nonstick, lightly oiled, or sprayed muffin cups.

Fill the shells with the filling, and bake for 15 minutes. Cool on a rack.

Makes 12 tarts

Per serving: Calories: 164, Protein: 1 gm., Fat: 3 gm., Carbohydrates: 31 gm.

Vegetarian Mincemeat Tarts

4 medium tart apples, peeled, cored,
   and chopped
1 c. raisins
⅔ c. frozen apple juice concentrate,
   thawed
½ c. dried currants
grated zest and juice of 1 medium
   orange
2 T. dark molasses
1 tsp. ground cinnamon
½ tsp. ground allspice
¼ tsp. EACH salt, ground nutmeg, and
   powdered ginger
1-2 T. brandy (optional)

To make the No-Sugar Vegetarian Mincemeat, place all the ingredients in a large pot. Bring this to a boil, then simmer, uncovered, over medium heat for about 15 minutes, or until the apples are tender and most of the juice has cooked down. Cool thoroughly before using (can be frozen).

Make tart shells as directed in the recipe for *Buttertarts.* Fill with Mincemeat and bake as directed for *Buttertarts.* Cool on a rack.

Makes 12 tarts

Per serving: Calories: 181, Protein: 2 gm., Fat: 3 gm., Carbohydrates: 35 gm.

Pumpkin Pie

I've been serving this pie for several years, and no one realizes that it's not only non-dairy but egg-free and very low in fat. It's very important to make this the day before you serve it, so that the filling can set properly.

Prepare ½ recipe of *Yeasted Pastry* Dough (p. 163) or ½ recipe of the *Low-Fat Oil Pastry* (p. 161). Roll it out to fit a lightly oiled, 9" pie pan, place it in the pan, and crimp the edges. Preheat the oven to 350°F.

To make the filling, mix the ingredients well in a blender. When the mixture is smooth, pour it into the prepared crust. Bake for 60 minutes, covering the edges of the pie crust with foil if they begin to brown too quickly. Cool on a rack, then refrigerate overnight before serving. Top with *Whipped Soy Cream Topping* (p. 168).

Serves 8

Per serving: Calories: 144, Protein: 3 gm., Fat: 0 gm., Carbohydrates: 33 gm.

Have ready:
½ recipe Yeasted Pastry Dough,
   (p. 163),
   or Low-Fat Oil Pastry (p. 161)

Filling
2 c. solid-pack, canned pumpkin, or
   cooked pumpkin, mashed and well-
   drained
1 c. reduced-fat soymilk or other non-
   dairy milk
¾ c. brown sugar or Sucanat,
   or ½ c. honey
¼ c. cornstarch
1 T. molasses or blackstrap molasses
1 tsp. ground cinnamon
1 tsp. pure vanilla extract
½ tsp. ground ginger
½ tsp. ground nutmeg
½ tsp. salt
¼ tsp. ground allspice or cloves

◆◆

"Ice Creams" and Whipped Topping for Desserts

There are now quite a few low-fat, vegan, non-dairy, frozen desserts (by law they aren't allowed to be called "ice creams") on the market, but, if you should have trouble finding one, here are two basic versions that you can make yourself—either in an ice cream maker, or simply with a freezer and a food processor or Champion juicer.

I also offer you a low-fat, whipped topping recipe and a pourable "cream" recipe. You can find some low-fat, vegan whipped toppings in your supermarket frozen food or refrigerator section. They aren't bad for special occasions, but they contain a lot of rather dubious ingredients, so you may prefer to make your own.

Rich Vanilla "Ice Cream"
for Ice Cream Makers

1 c. cold water mixed with ¾ tsp. agar powder (or 1½ T. flakes)

1 (10.5 oz.) pkg. reduced-fat, firm or extra-firm, SILKEN tofu
¾ c. reduced-fat soy or other non-dairy milk
½ c. sugar or alternate sweetener, or ⅓ c. honey
½ T. pure vanilla extract
¼ tsp. salt

In a small saucepan, simmer the agar and water for 3-5 minutes. Add to a blender with the remaining ingredients, and combine until very smooth. Freeze according to the directions for your machine.

Let the "ice cream" thaw out a bit before you serve it, to soften it up a bit.

Maple Variation: Omit sugar or honey and non-dairy milk, and use *1¼ cup pure maple syrup.*

Makes 3½ cups

Per cup: Calories: 160, Protein: 7 gm., Fat: 1 gm., Carbohydrates: 31 gm.

Basic Tofu "Ice Cream"
for a Food Processor or Juicer

Combine the ingredients in a blender or food processor until *very* smooth. Freeze the mixture in a flat pan. Just before serving, break the mixture into chunks, and run it through either a food processor or a Champion juicer with the blank in place until creamy. Serve immediately.

Maple Variation: Use the medium-firm tofu, and omit the sugar or honey and the ½ cup water. Use *1¼ cups pure maple syrup* instead.

Makes about 1¾ cups

Per cup: Calories: 173, Protein: 12 gm., Fat: 2 gm., Carbohydrates: 28 gm.

---

2 (10.5 oz.) pkgs. reduced-fat, firm
   SILKEN tofu, drained,
   or 1 lb. reduced-fat, medium-firm,
   regular tofu + ½ c. water
½ c. sugar or alternate sweetener,
   dissolved in 2 T. water,
   or ⅓ c. honey
1 T. pure vanilla extract
⅛ tsp. salt

◆◆◆

Whipped Soy Cream Topping

This is a simple recipe with a rich, clean taste—no dissolving agar or beating with electric egg beaters. For best results, make it up the day before serving. The coconut extract doesn't make it taste like coconut—it just lends a certain richness to the mixture.

⅔ c. reduced-fat, extra-firm, SILKEN tofu, crumbled
⅓ c. reduced-fat, commercial rice milk, almond milk, or soymilk (plain or vanilla)
2-3 tsp. honey,
   or 4-6 tsp. light sugar or alternate sweetener
¼ tsp. coconut extract
pinch salt (optional)

Place all the ingredients in a blender or food processor, and blend until *very* smooth. Place in a covered container, and refrigerate for several hours or, preferably, overnight.

To vary the flavors, you can use *1 tablespoon brandy, rum, or flavored liqueur of choice* in place of 1 tablespoon liquid. If you want a maple-flavored topping, omit the honey or sugar and 1 tablespoon of the liquid. Add *2 tablespoons maple syrup.*

Makes about 1 cup

Per 2 Tbsp.: Calories: 18, Protein: 1 gm., Fat: 0 gm., Carbohydrates: 3 gm.

Pourable Soy Cream

Fllow the recipe for *Whipped Soy Cream Topping,* but use ½ cup crumbled, silken tofu and ½ cup rice (or other) milk. If you use soft, silken tofu, this will be like a cereal cream. If you use firm or extra-firm, silken tofu, it will be like a thick pouring cream to use on cobblers and crisps.

The Basics

This section contains basic recipes that are called for in many of the menus in this book, but could be used in your everyday, low-fat cooking as well. Included are main dish staples, using seitan, tofu, and textured vegetable protein, as well as sauces and condiments.

About Textured Vegetable Protein

Textured vegetable protein is a low-fat, dry product, used as a meat substitute. It is made from soy flour, cooked under pressure, then extruded to make different sizes and shapes. It has the advantage of being lower in fat than tofu and can take the place of frozen tofu in many recipes. Even if you object to the use of "meat substitutes" on a regular basis, textured vegetable protein can be a great transition food for people who were raised on meat and, despite the best of motives and intentions, miss their familiar foods and textures.

Textured vegetable protein will keep for a long time, has no cholesterol, has almost *no fat* and sodium, and is an excellent source of protein and fiber. It is easily rehydrated for use in soups, stews, casseroles, and sauces. The most common form available is granules, which have a ground meat-like texture. They are excellent in chilies and spaghetti sauces and can be made into burgers and "sausage" patties, (see p. 171). I use them in egg rolls and cabbage rolls too. Textured vegetable protein can also be found in the form of flakes and chunks. All these types can be ordered by mail (see p. 186).

Reconstituted textured vegetable protein can be made ahead of time and refrigerated for several days or frozen for future use. The *granules* are quickly rehydrated by mixing with almost an equal amount of boiling liquid, covering, and setting aside for 5 minutes. Boiling water is usually used for reconstituting, but broth or tomato juice can also be used. The rule is, for each cup of textured vegetable protein granules use ⅞ cup liquid (yields 1⅓ cups reconstituted).

When I'm substituting for meat in a recipe, I always figure that 1 lb. of meat is equal to about 2 cups of reconstituted granules or frozen tofu in volume.

Vegetarian "Ground Pork"

This is a very versatile mixture which I use often for things such as won ton and other Oriental dumplings, egg rolls, etc. You can cook it first and crumble it, or use it uncooked.

---

1 c. dry textured vegetable protein granules

¾ c. boiling water

2 T. soy sauce

4 oz. reduced-fat, firm or medium-firm tofu, mashed

½ c. pure gluten powder (vital wheat gluten)

In a medium bowl, mix together the textured vegetable protein, water, and soy sauce. Let this soak for 10 minutes, then add the tofu and mix together well. Let the mixture cool thoroughly (if you don't, the gluten will clump into strings). To speed this up, you can spread the mixture on a plate, and place it in the freezer for a few minutes. Add the gluten powder and mix well with your hands.

To cook the mixture, form it into 8-10 thin patties. To *pan-fry*, heat two large, nonstick or lightly oiled, heavy frying pans over medium heat. Add the patties, cover, and cook 7 minutes (10 minutes if you want them browned). Turn the patties over and cook 7-10 minutes on the other side. *To bake*, place the patties on a nonstick or lightly oiled cookie sheet, cover tightly with foil, and bake at 400°F for 7 minutes (10 minutes, if you want them browned). Turn them over and bake 7-10 minutes longer (cover again if you want the mixture to stay moist). Refrigerate or freeze for future use.

Baking is a good method if you want to double or triple the recipe and freeze it.

Makes the equivilant of 1 lb. (8 to 10 patties)

Per patty: Calories: 84, Protein: 14 gm., Fat: 1 gm., Carbohydrates: 5 gm.

◆◆

Vegetarian"Burger"

This mixture makes tasty "burgers" and is also useful as a substitute for cooked hamburger in many recipes.

Follow the recipe for *Vegetarian "Ground Pork,"* but use *1 T. soy sauce* and *1 T. yeast extract (Marmite)* instead of the 2 T. soy sauce. Along with the tofu add *1 T. ketchup, 1 tsp. Kitchen Bouquet or Vegetarian Worcestershire Sauce (p. 176) 1 tsp. dried marjoram, ½ tsp. EACH garlic granules, onion powder, and dried thyme,* and *freshly ground black pepper to taste.* Make into 8 patties.

Makes the equivalent of 1 lb. hamburger or 8 to 10 patties

Per patty: Calories: 84, Protein: 14 gm., Fat: 1 gm., Carbohydrates: 5 gm.

Vegetarian "Sausage"

Make the *Vegetarian "Ground Pork,"* adding along with the tofu: *2 tsp. crumbled sage leaves, 1 tsp. dried marjoram, ½ tsp. EACH garlic granules, onion powder, thyme, salt, and red pepper flakes,* freshly ground black pepper to taste, and *1 tsp. liquid smoke (optional).*

Make 10 thin patties or 20 small sausage "links," and cook according to either method as directed in the basic recipe until browned on all sides (7-10 minutes per side for patties; 5 minutes per side—4 sides—for "links").

Makes 10 patties or "links"

Per patty: Calories: 61, Protein: 9 gm., Fat: 1 gm., Carbohydrates: 5 gm.

Vegetarian "Chorizo"

This spicy version is delicious with Spanish and Mexican foods.

Make the *Vegetarian"Ground Pork,"* using only ½ cup boiling water and adding, along with the soy sauce: *2 T. red wine vinegar, 2 T. dry red wine, 1 T. EACH chile powder and paprika, 1 tsp. EACH salt, onion powder,* and *dried oregano, ½ tsp. EACH garlic granules and ground cumin,* and *¼ tsp. ground cinnamon.* Instead of ½ cup pure gluten powder, use only ¼ cup and add *2 T. unbleached flour* with the tofu.

Form and cook as for *Vegetarian "Sausage"* above.

Makes 10 patties or "links"

Per patty: Calories: 61, Protein: 9 gm., Fat: 1 gm., Carbohydrates: 5 gm.

◆◇◆

Pan-Fried "Breast of Tofu"

This is a staple in my house. I call it "breast of tofu," because it takes the place of chicken breast in sandwiches, stir-fries, salads, and many other dishes.

Breast of Tofu Marinade
1½ cups water
¼ cup soy sauce
3 Tbsp. nutritional yeast flakes
2 tsp. dried sage leaves, crumbled,
    or 1 tsp. ground sage
½ tsp. dried rosemary
½ tsp. dried thyme
½ tsp. onion powder

1½-2 lbs. reduced-fat, extra-firm or
    pressed, regular tofu

Makes 32 slices

Per slice: Calories: 41, Protein: 6 gm. Fat: 1 gm., Carbohydrates: 2 gm.

Prepare Breast of Tofu Marinade by combining the water, soy sauce, nutritional yeast, and spices in a 2-quart bowl

Instead of all or some of the traditional "poultry seasonings" (thyme, sage, etc.), use cumin, coriander, basil, oregano, or whatever herbs are suitable for the dish you are making. For spicy Breast of Tofu, add as much Louisiana-style hot sauce to the marinade as you like.

Cut the tofu into ¼-inch thick slices. Marinate for as little as a few hours or as long as two weeks (in the refrigerator). Turn the slices, spoon over the marinade from time to time, or store in a tightly lidded container, and shake.

Simply "pan-fry" as many slices as you need in a nonstick pan over medium heat until browned on both sides. Use immediately or cool on racks and refrigerate. The wrapped slices will keep well in the refrigerator for several days.

Smoky Pan-Fried Tofu

This variation is great for stir-fries, enchiladas, casseroles, etc.

Mix ¾ cup water, 2 T. soy sauce, and ½ tsp. liquid smoke together, and pour over the tofu slices in a plastic container with a tight lid. Let marinate for at least 12 hours, or several days. Pan-fry as for Breast of Tofu, using half the tofu called for.

Makes 16 slices

Per slice: Calories: 38, Protein: 6 gm. Fat: 1 gm., Carbohydrates: 2 gm.

Beefy Seitan Roast

This is excellent hot or sliced cold for sandwiches. Make the whole recipe and use the leftovers for sandwiches, or grind some in a meat grinder or food processor for "hamburger." Cut some of it into strips for stir-fries and stroganoff, and/or cut thicker slices for "steaks" or "cutlets" to pan fry, grill, or broil (with or without a breading and with or without a salt-free grilling sauce, barbecue sauce, or marinade). Use the leftover cooking broth to enhance sauces.

In a dry bowl, mix the gluten powder, nutritional yeast, onion powder, garlic, and black pepper together. In a smaller bowl, whisk together the first batch of cold water or mushroom broth, ketchup, soy sauce, yeast extract, and Kitchen Bouquet.

Pour the broth into the gluten mixture, and mix it into a ball. Place the ball into a roasting pan with a cover large enough to allow the ball to double (press the ball down to flatten a bit).

Preheat the oven to 350°F. Prepare a cooking broth made by mixing together the remaining ingredients. Pour over the gluten ball, and bake uncovered for ½ hour. Prick the roast all over with a fork, and turn it over. Lower heat to 300°F and bake covered for 1 more hour, turning once in a while.

Slow-Cooker Method: Cook in a slow-cooker on HIGH for 10 hours.

Serves 6 to 8

Per serving: Calories: 181, Protein: 34 gm., Fat: 1 gm., Carbohydrates: 9 gm.

2 c. instant gluten powder (vital wheat gluten)
2 T. nutritional yeast flakes
1 tsp. onion powder
½ tsp. garlic granules
black pepper to taste

1½ c. cold water,
  or broth from soaking Chinese dried mushrooms
2 T. ketchup
2 T. soy sauce or mushroom soy sauce
2 tsp. Marmite or other yeast extract, or dark miso
2 tsp. Kitchen Bouquet

4 c. water or broth from soaking dried Chinese mushrooms
¼ c. ketchup
¼ c. soy sauce or mushroom soy sauce
4 tsp. Marmite or other yeast extract, or dark miso
4 tsp. Kitchen Bouquet

Tofu Mayonnaise

Silken *tofu makes a smooth, thick, rich-tasting mayonnaise that doesn't separate easily and needs no oil.*

1 (10.5 oz.) pkg. reduced-fat, extra-firm
    or firm, SILKEN tofu
1½ T. cider vinegar or lemon juice
1 tsp. sweetener of your choice (optional)
1 tsp. salt
½ tsp. dry mustard
⅛ tsp. white pepper

Combine all the ingredients in a blender until very smooth. This will keep about 2 weeks in the refrigerator.

Makes 1⅓ cups

Per 2 Tbsp: Calories: 13, Protein: 2 gm., Fat: 0 gm., Carbohydrates: 1 gm.

Tofu Sour Cream

You'll *find yourself using this mixture over and over again. It's creamy and rich-tasting, just like the real thing, yet the whole recipe contains less than 7 grams of fat (made with regular silken tofu). You can use it just like dairy sour cream, in dips, dressings, and cooking.*

1 (10.5 oz.) pkg. reduced-fat, extra-firm,
    SILKEN tofu
1-2 T. lemon juice
1½ tsp. light miso,
    or ¼ tsp. salt
½ tsp. sugar or 1 tsp. alternate sweetener

1 T. white vinegar,
    or 1,000-2,000 mg. crushed vitamin C,
    or ¼-½ tsp. ascorbic acid (optional—
    for more tang)

Place all ingredients in a food processor. Process until very smooth. Store in a covered container in the refrigerator for up to a week.

Please note: The white vinegar, ascorbic acid, or vitamin C gives the mixture the tangy sourness of sour cream without having to add so much liquid that it thins out the mixture—use whichever amount suits your taste. Ascorbic acid powder is available in pharmacies.

Makes about 1⅓ cups

Per 2 Tbsp: Calories: 26, Protein: 3 gm., Fat: 1 gm., Carbohydrates: 1 gm

Tofu "Yogurt"

Use only ½ tsp. miso or a pinch of salt, and use 2-4 T. *of lemon juice.* Omit vinegar, vitamin C, or ascorbic acid. If you like, add some non-dairy acidophilous powder, available in health food stores.

Tofu "Feta"

Cut the tofu into cubes or slices. Combine the remaining ingredients to make a marinade, and mix in the tofu.

Keep this refrigerated in a covered jar for up to three weeks, shaking the jar every day. Use in salads.

Makes 2 cups

Per ½ cup: Calories: 120, Protein: 12 gm., Fat: 2 gm., Carbohydrates: 12 gm

1 lb. reduced-fat, extra-firm, regular or SILKEN tofu

1 c. water
½ c. light miso
2 T. lemon juice or white wine vinegar
1 tsp. salt

Herbed Tofu "Feta"

Add to the marinade *2 bay leaves, 2 cloves peeled garlic, 2 dried red chile peppers, and ½ tsp. EACH dried thyme and rosemary.* This version is an excellent addition to an antipasto plate.

Sesame Meal

I *use this roasted sesame product for the unique, almost smoky taste usually provided by Chinese sesame oil. Ground sesame meal, however, provides more fiber with less fat. For each tablespoon of sesame oil or tahini called for in a recipe, I substitute a tablespoon of Sesame Meal.*

Place the seeds in a heavy, dry skillet over high heat. Stir constantly until the seeds turn golden-beige and start to pop. Remove them from the heat, and pour them into a blender. Blend at high speed, stopping to stir from the bottom a few times, until they are the consistency of a fine meal, but not a paste. Keep in a covered container in the freezer.

2 c. hulled, raw sesame seeds

Makes a generous 2 cups

Per Tbsp: Calories: 47, Protein: 2 gm., Fat: 5 gm., Carbohydrates: 1 gm

Vegetarian Worcestershire Sauce

1 c. cider vinegar
⅓ c. dark molasses
¼ c. soy sauce or mushroom soy sauce
¼ c. water
3 T. lemon juice
1½ T. salt
1½ tsp. powdered mustard
1 tsp. onion powder
¾ tsp. ground ginger
½ tsp. black pepper
¼ tsp. garlic granules
¼ tsp. cayenne pepper
¼ tsp. ground cinnamon
⅛ tsp. ground cloves or allspice
⅛ tsp. ground cardamom

Combine all the ingredients in a blender. Pour into a saucepan and bring to a boil. Store in a jar in the refrigerator.

Makes about 2 cups

Per Tbsp.: Calories: 10, Protein: 0 gm., Fat: 0 gm., Carbohydrates: 3 gm.

Dry-Roasted Soybeans ("Soynuts") and Chickpeas

Keep a supply of both of these on hand in the freezer to use for snacks or in recipes in place of nuts and seeds.

Soak dry soybeans or chickpeas in enough water to cover overnight. Drain, rinse, and place in a pot with enough fresh water to cover. Bring to a boil, turn down, and simmer for 10 minutes. Drain.

Spread the beans in a single layer on lightly oiled cookie sheets. Roast at 350°F for about 45 minutes or until golden and crispy all over, stirring several times while roasting. Cool thoroughly, then store in plastic bags or containers in the freezer.

◇◇

Guilt-Free
Bread Spread

This is an easier version of my Corn Butter recipe from The Almost No-Fat Cookbook. It has a nice mild flavor and melts nicely on vegetables.

In a small saucepan, mix together the water and cornstarch. Stir the mixture over high heat constantly until it is thickened and clear. Place it in the blender or food processor with the other ingredients, and blend until very smooth. Place in an airtight container and refrigerate. It keeps only about a week.

You can make half the recipe, but you will have to use a food processor to make this small amount successfully.

Makes about 1½ cups

Per Tbsp.: Calories: 7, Protein: 1 gm., Fat: 0 gm., Carbohydrates: 1 gm.

1 c. cold water
2 T. cornstarch (this doesn't work well with other starches)
⅔ c. reduced-fat, medium-firm, regular tofu
4 tsp. light tofu beverage mix (or other good-tasting plain, non-dairy beverage powder—NOT bulk soymilk powder)
1 tsp. lemon juice
¾ tsp. salt
⅛ tsp. paprika
⅛ tsp. turmeric

Garlic Spread

Add ½ T. nutritional yeast flakes, 2 cloves peeled garlic, ½ tsp. onion powder, ½ tsp. dried herb of choice, and ¼ tsp. more salt.

Mock Hollandaise Sauce

Use 2 cups of water, 2 tsp. salt, and 2 T. lemon juice. Add 1 T. nutritional yeast flakes, 1 tsp. onion powder, and ¼ tsp. garlic granules. You can also add 1 tsp. dried herbs, ground cumin, or chipotle chile paste for extra flavor, if you like.

Roasting or Grilling Marinade

This very versatile marinade coats vegetables or potato wedges and both flavors and browns them in the oven. The result is very much like vegetables that are roasted or grilled with oil. Oven-baked "chips" are crunchy and golden; roasted vegetables are juicy and glazed. The marinade also works well as a coating for making crispy croutons. I keep a jar of it in my refrigerator at all times.

For certain things you might want the stronger flavor of wine vinegar, cider or balsamic vinegar, or gourmet fruit vinegar instead of the lemon juice, but lemon juice is the most versatile. You can use fruit juice for some of the liquid, if you wish, or orange zest instead of the lemon zest. For a sweet glaze on root vegetables, add 2 tablespoons of maple syrup, honey, or other sweetener to ½ cup of the marinade.

2 c. cold water
2 T. cornstarch
2 T. chicken-style vegetarian broth, or 2 vegetarian broth cubes

¾ c. lemon juice
grated zest of 1 lemon
2 T. herbal salt
4 large cloves garlic, crushed
1 tsp. dried oregano or other herb of choice, or 1 T. fresh herbs

In a heavy saucepan, mix the cold water, cornstarch, and vegetable broth. Cook, stirring constantly, over high heat until the mixture has thickened and come to a boil. Add the remaining ingredients.

Cut the vegetables into even-sized pieces. To grill, steam firm vegetables until half cooked. Marinate the vegetables for 4-6 hours before broiling or grilling. To roast, coat the vegetables well with the marinade. Roast in a shallow baking pan at 400°F for 45-60 minutes, turning the vegetables occasionally.

Makes about 3 cups

Per ½ cup: Calories: 18, Protein: 0 gm., Fat: 0 gm., Carbohydrates: 4 gm.

Croutons

Combine 2½ cups bread cubes with ¼ cup marinade. Bake on a cookie sheet at 350°F until golden and crispy.

No-Oil Granola

*T*his makes a great substitute for nuts in baking, as well as a breafast cereal. Try to use the coconut extract–it lends a very rich flavor to the granola. This small batch can be made very quickly and easily, with no fear of burning, in the microwave.

Preheat the oven to 250°F. Mix the ingredients together well with your hands, and spread the mixture onto a nonstick, lightly oiled or sprayed cookie sheet. Bake for 20 minutes, then stir the mixture every 5 minutes for the next 15-20 minutes to prevent burning. When the granola is lightly browned, it should be ready. Cool the granola thoroughly before storing in an airtight container.

 To cook in a microwave, cover the carousel of a large microwave with a layer of waxed paper. Spread the granola mix evenly over the waxed paper. Cook on HIGH for 3 minutes. Stir the granola and spread it out evenly again. Cook on HIGH 3 more minutes, then let stand 3 minutes before scraping it onto a cookie sheet to cool.

 You can add ½ c. dried fruit for breakfast cereal, if you wish.

> 2 c. rolled oats or other flaked hot cereal
> ¾ c. whole wheat flour or other whole grain flour
> ½ c. wheat bran or other cereal bran
> ⅓ c. maple syrup or alternate syrup (not honey)
> ¼ tsp. coconut extract (or pure almond extract)
> ¼ tsp. salt
> ¼ tsp. ground cinnamon

Makes 3¼ cups

Per ½ cup: Calories: 203, Protein: 7 gm., Fat: 2 gm., Carbohydrates: 38 gm.

Homemade Tortilla Chips

*T*ortilla chips can be made quickly and easily in the microwave with no fear of burning. To make them from frozen tortillas, carefully separate 3 frozen corn tortillas without breaking them. Cut each tortilla into 8 wedges with scissors. Lay the wedges, not touching, on two layers of paper towelling right on top of a large microwave carousel. Salt if desired. Cook on HIGH for 1½ minutes.

Per 8 chips: Calories: 65, Protein: 2 gm., Fat: 1 gm., Carbohydrates: 12 gm.

Vegetarian Antipasto Relish

This Italian-style relish, usually made with seafood and olives, is popular in Canada, and it makes excellent hostess gifts as well as a great appetizer with crackers. This no-fat version is delicious!

1¼ c. Roasting and Grilling Marinade (p. 178),
  or a commercial fat-free vinaigrette dressing
4 c. canned (drained) or steam-fried mushrooms, sliced
1 lb. cauliflower, cut into small pieces
2 bunches green onions, chopped

4 (6 oz.) cans tomato paste mixed with water to make 7¾ c.
8-9 large green bell peppers, seeded and chopped
2 lbs. frozen, small, whole green beans, thawed
⅔ c. honey,
  or 1 c. sugar or alternate sweetener

¾ c. apple cider vinegar
4 tsp. liquid hot pepper seasoning
4 tsp. salt
1 tsp. kelp powder, if you miss the seafood taste (optional)

1 large eggplant, peeled, sliced and grilled until soft, then chopped (you need about 2 c. chopped, cooked eggplant)
¼ c. light miso

In a large, non-aluminum pot, boil together the *Roasting and Grilling Marinade* or vinaigrette, the mushrooms, cauliflower, and green onions for 2 minutes. Add the tomato paste and water, green peppers, green beans, and honey or sugar. Boil 2 more minutes.

Add the vinegar, liquid hot pepper seasoning, and salt (and kelp powder, if using). Boil 2-5 more minutes. Stir in the eggplant and miso, and mix well.

Pack the antipasto into 16 half-pint canning jars or freezer containers, and cover tightly. Freeze the antipasto, or waterbath-can the jars for 15 minutes.

Makes 16 half-pint jars

Per ½ cup: Calories: 66, Protein: 1 gm., Fat: 0 gm., Carbohydrates: 14 gm.

◆◆

Simple No-Fat Vinaigrette Dressing

In a small saucepan, mix together the broth and cornstarch over high heat, stirring constantly until thickened and clear. Add the remaining ingredients and pour the mixture into a cruet or covered jar. Refrigerate.

Makes about 1¼ cups

Per Tbsp.: Calories: 4, Protein: 0 gm., Fat: 0 gm., Carbohydrates: 0 gm.

> 1 c. light vegetarian broth
> 2 tsp. cornstarch
>
> ¼ c. wine vinegar
> 1 T. Dijon mustard
> ½ T. honey or alternate sweetener
> 1 clove garlic, crushed
> 1 tsp. salt or herbal salt
> 1 tsp. dried basil or other herb (or 1 T. chopped fresh herb)
> ¼ tsp. paprika

Wine-Marinated Dried Tomatoes

If you love dried tomatoes packed in olive oil with herbs, try this delicious, fat-free recipe. It makes a great appetizer as part of an antipasto platter too.

Mix the broth and cornstarch in a small saucepan, and stir constantly over high heat until it thickens and clears. Mix in the remaining ingredients, and pour into a sterilized pint jar. Seal tightly and refrigerate. Shake the jar at least once a day. The tomatoes are ready when they are no longer tough and chewy. Refrigerated, they will keep for about a month. Multiply the recipe as needed.

Makes 1 pint jar

Per ¼ cup: Calories: 48, Protein: 1 gm., Fat: 0 gm., Carbohydrates: 8 gm.

> ½ c. light vegetarian broth mixed with 1 tsp. cornstarch
> 3 oz. dried tomatoes
> ½ c. dry red wine (or balsamic vinegar, or a mixture)
> 2 cloves garlic, peeled and minced
> 1 tsp. salt
> 1 bay leaf
> ½ tsp. dried thyme or rosemary, or a sprig of fresh thyme or rosemary
> ¼ tsp. dried basil, oregano or marjoram
> freshly ground black pepper to taste

Glossary

AGAR: Also known as agar-agar or kanten (the Japanese word), this vegetarian gelling agent is made from a seaweed. Like gelatin, it is tasteless and has no calories (but will set at room temperature), so it can be used instead of gelatin in fruit gels and savory aspic. It is widely available in natural food stores in the form of powder, flakes, or bars.

To gel 2 cups of liquid use 1 teaspoon of agar powder, or 2 tablespoons of agar flakes, or about half a bar of kanten. As a comparison, a tablespoon or packet of unflavored, regular gelatin will gel 2 cups of liquid. To use agar flakes instead of agar powder in a recipe, use six times as much.

Certain things interfere with the gelling of agar—vinegar and oxalic acid (found in chocolate and spinach), for instance. Fruit acids may soften the gel somewhat—you'll have to experiment with fruit juices to see if you need more than the recommended amount to achieve the degree of firmness that you like. Try using half again as much, especially with citrus, tomato, and pineapple.

BULGUR WHEAT: This quick-cooking wheat product is of ancient origin. Wheat kernels are boiled, dried, and cracked. The resulting bulgur needs only to be cooked for 10 to 15 minutes (1 part bulgur to 2 parts liquid).

EGG REPLACER: Most of the time, eggs can be eliminated or replaced by tofu, soymilk, or cornstarch, but sometimes a commercial egg replacer works best. I use EnerG Egg Replacer, which comes in powdered form and is made from potato and tapioca starches, calcium, citric acid, and carbohydrate gum. Half a tablespoon beaten with 2 tablespoons of water replaces one egg in most baking recipes. Recipes on the box give directions for replacing egg yolks, beaten egg whites, etc.

INSTANT GLUTEN FLOUR: Instant gluten powder (also known as vital wheat gluten, "Do-Pep," or pure gluten flour) is available in most natural food stores. The powder is made from gluten, the protein in wheat. Small amounts can be added to breads to improve it for bread-baking, or it can be mixed with cold liquid to make meat substitutes. The raw gluten is cooked in a flavored broth and is then known by the Japanese name *seitan*.

Do not confuse instant gluten powder with something called "gluten flour." This product is refined wheat flour with gluten powder added. Make sure that it is vital wheat gluten that you are buying.

LIQUID SMOKE: This is a useful flavoring to replace the smoky taste of ham, bacon, etc., especially in bean dishes. New studies show that it does not contain carcinogenic impurities, as once thought.

MISO: Miso is a Japanese fermented soybean and grain (usually rice or barley) paste which is used as a soup base and a flavoring. It is salty but highly nutritious and valued for its digestive qualities. Unpasteurized miso contains beneficial bacteria similar to that in yogurt, so avoid heating it to the boiling point. If your natural foods store has a selection of misos, try them out to see which you like—there can be a number of varieties: dark, light, sweet, mellow, etc. When I call for miso, I'm referring to light brown rice or barley miso.

NUTRITIONAL YEAST: Nutritional yeast is NOT the same thing as brewer's yeast or baking yeast. Nutritional yeast flakes have a cheesy taste and, when mixed with soy sauce or spices, also a rather "chickeny" taste, so they are best used in savory dishes. I also use it in some baking to replace the rich taste of egg yolk.

Yeast is a concentrated source of protein, B-vitamins (some brands have vitamin B-12 added), and minerals, and contains no fat and few calories, so it is an important seasoning in vegan cooking. You might like to keep some on your table, like salt, for sprinkling on foods (delicious on popcorn!). You'll find it in natural foods stores.

OAT FLOUR: In some baking recipes, a low-gluten flour, such as *oat flour*, is required. You can use rice, millet, barley, or other low-gluten flours if you prefer, but oats are common in most households and can be made into flour easily and inexpensively in your blender. Simply process rolled or quick oatmeal in your *dry* blender until it is the consistency of flour. Store the flour in a tightly-covered container in your freezer.

RICE: Whenever possible, use brown rice. It is superior to white rice in terms of fiber and nutrients. Long grain brown rice cooks up in fluffy, separate grains—short grain is stickier. There are some delicious varieties of brown rice besides these—brown basmati, Calmati, or Texmati, which are very long-grained and aromatic, and wehani, a rust-colored, long grain brown rice with a popcorn aroma and the appearance of wild rice. It's good mixed with regular, long grain brown.

If you prefer white rice, use either white basmati, which is not only delicious, but is not polished, or converted (parboiled) rice, which is steamed before hulling, so that some of the nutrients from the bran are forced into the kernel. Under no circumstances use instant white rice.

To avoid mushy rice, use 1 part rice to 1½ parts water. The Spanish sauté their rice in a little hot oil before adding the liquid—I do this in a dry pan, which also results in dry separate grains. Another way to ensure non-sticky rice is to add it very slowly to boiling water. More sticky, Oriental-style rice is started in cold water.

Both brown and white rice should be brought to a boil, then covered, turned to low heat, and simmered until done without lifting the lid or stirring. The lid should fit tightly, and the pot should have a heavy bottom. White rice cooks in 15-20 minutes, brown rice in 45 minutes. Both improve from standing off the heat with the lid on for 10 minutes.

For *quick-cooking brown rice*, soak the brown rice in its cooking water for at least 4 hours (before you go to work, for instance). After soaking, it will cook in 20 minutes!

SOYMILK POWDER: Soymilk powder is excellent for adding a little extra protein to baked goods. Do not confuse it with soy flour, which hasn't undergone the same amount of cooking that soy powder has. You can find inexpensive brands in bulk in natural foods stores or more expensive varieties that are suitable for mixing up as beverages, as well as for baking.

SOY SAUCE (SHOYU, TAMARI): You'll notice that I use soy sauce in many non-Oriental recipes. It has a meaty, rich flavor that adds body to many recipes. Do not purchase cheap soy sauce that contains hydrolized vegetable protein and caramel coloring. Most supermarkets carry excellent, inexpensive brands of naturally fermented Chinese and Japanese soy sauce. The label should state that it contains only soybeans, salt, water, and sometimes wheat. Some manufacturers make "lite" varieties that contain less salt.

If you have a problem with yeast sensitivities in fermented foods, you can also use liquid aminos for this purpose.

TOFU (BEAN CURD, SOYBEAN CURD): Tofu comes in many forms—regular (medium-firm, firm, or extra-firm [or pressed]), soft, silken (soft, firm, or extra-firm), marinated, frozen, freeze-dried, and fried. The varieties most often called for in this book are reduced-fat, firm or medium-firm regular, and reduced-fat (or "lite"), firm or extra-firm silken. The regular styles are available in bulk or in vacuum-packaged plastic tubs in many supermarket produce departments and most natural foods stores (the vacuum packs need to be refrigerated and have a "best before" date stamped on them). Soft, firm, and extra-firm silken tofu comes in tetra packs weighing 10.5 oz. and does not need refrigerating until opening. The packs can be stored for about a year, making them great emergency and camping food. Silken tofu has a very creamy, smooth quality with little soy taste, making it excellent for blended dairy substitutes, but it is more expensive than the regular type.

Fresh bulk tofu, or any packaged tofu that has been opened must be kept covered with water in the refrigerator, and the water must be changed daily. It will last a week or two this way. After that time it's best to freeze it in plastic bags (tub tofu can be frozen right in the package).

YEAST EXTRACT: This dark, salty paste with a "beefy" flavor is popular as a spread in England and Australia, but more often is used as a broth base in North America. Since it is made from nutritional yeast, it is rich in nutrients. I find the flavor very strong, but if used sparingly in stews and other dishes it provides a distinctive, beefy flavor—I usually mix it with soy sauce. You can find it in the soup or spice section of some supermarkets, natural foods, or specialty foods stores under various brand names, such as Marmite, Vegemite, Vegex, Sovex, and Savorex.

Bibliography

For in-depth information about low-fat, vegetarian diets and nutrition, and vegetarian diets for children:

Barnard, Neal, M.D., *Food for Life: How the New Four Food Groups Can Save Your Life*, Harmony Books, N.Y., 1993.

Elliot, Rose, *Vegetarian Mother and Baby Book*, Pantheon Books, N.Y., 1986.

Klaper, Michael, M.D., *Vegan Nutrition Pure and Simple* and *Pregnancy, Children and the Vegan Diet*, Gentle World, 1987.

Messina, Mark, PhD, and Messina, Virginia, RD., *The Simple Soybean and Your Health*, Avery, Garden City Park, N.Y., 1994.

Ornish, Dean, M.D., *Eat More, Weigh Less*, HarperCollins, N.Y., 1993, also *Dr. Dean Ornish's Program for Reversing Heart Disease*, Random House, N.Y., 1990.

Robbins, John, *Diet for a New America*, Stillpoint, Walpole, N.H., 1987.

For more information on specific holidays:

Drucker, Malk, *Hanukkah: Eight Nights, Eight Lights*, Holiday House, N.Y., 1980.

Folklore of World Holidays, ed. by Margaret Read MacDonald, Gale Research, Inc., Detroit/London, 1991.

Kozodoy, Ruth, *The Book of Jewish Holidays*, Behrman House, Inc. N.Y., 1981.

McClester, Cedris, *Kwanzaa, Rev. Ed.*, Gumbs and Thomas Pub., Inc., 1993.

Parry, Caroline, *Let's Celebrate!*, Kids Can Press, Toronto, 1987.

Rockland, Mae Shafter, *The Jewish Party Book*, Schoken Books, N.Y., 1978.

Visser, Margaret, *Much Depends on Dinner*, McClelland and Stewart, Toronto, 1986.

Watson, Jane Werner, *India Celebrates!*, Garrard Pub., Champaign, Ill., 1974

For cookbooks on holiday celebrations:

Chelf, Vicky Rae and Biscotti, Dominique, *The Sensuous Vegetarian Barbecue*, Avery Pub., Garden City Park, N.Y., 1994.

Copage, Eric V., *Kwanzaa*, Quill/William Morrow, N.Y., 1991.

Field, Carol, *Celebrating Italy*, William Morrow, N.Y., 1990.

Machlin, Edna Servi, *The Classic Cuisine of the Italian Jews*, Everest House, N.Y., 1981.

McCune, Kelly, *Vegetables on the Grill*, Harper Perennial, N.Y., 1992.

Nathan, Joan, *The Jewish Holiday Kitchen*, Shocken Books, N.Y., 1979.

Sheraton, Mimi, *Visions of Sugarplums, Rev. Exp. Ed.*, Harper and Row, N.Y., 1986.

Schumann, Kate and Messina, Virginia, MPH and RD, *Vegetarian No-Cholesterol Barbecue Cookbook*, St. Martins, N.Y., 1994.

Simonds, Nina, *Chinese Seasons*, Houghton Mifflin Co., Boston, 1986.

Theoharous, Anne, *Cooking and Baking the Greek Way*, Holt, Rinehart and Winston, N.Y., 1977.

Time-Life, *Foods of the World* Series.

Wasserman, Debra, *The Lowfat Jewish Vegetarian Cookbook*, Vegetarian Resource Group, Baltimore, Md., 1994.

Wasserman, Debra, *No Cholesterol Passover Recipes, Rev. Ed.*, Vegetarian Resource Group, Baltimore, Md., 1995.

◇◇

Mail Order Sources

If you have a hard time finding certain specialty ingredients in your community, try some of the mail order sources below, or see if your public library has a catalog of mail order sources. Remember that many health or natural food stores carry such ethnic products as Vietnamese rice papers, poppadoms, and miso.

Alternately, consult the yellow pages in the phone book of your nearest large city (the library or phone company will have this.) Check under Food Products, Grocers, and Importers. You may find sources also under Health Foods or Natural Foods, and Oriental Goods. Some yellow pages have listings such as Mexican Foods, Chinese Foods, Japanese Foods, Asian Foods, Soybean Products, etc. Some of these retailers may be willing to ship within certain areas.

If you cannot find a particular product after exhausting all of these resources, please write to me care of the Book Publishing Company, Summertown, TN, 38483, and I will do my best to locate a source for you.

Sources are arranged geographically.

Dean and DeLuca Retail and Mail Order Dept.
560 Broadway
New York, NY 10012
(212) 431-1691
beans, Mediterranean foods, specialty foods, equipment, books—has catalog

Zabar's
2245 Broadway
New York, NY 10024
(212) 496-1234
hard-to-find specialty ingredients

Paprika Weiss
1572 Second Ave.
New York, NY 10028
(212) 288-6117
huge supply of spices, beans, equipment, etc.—great catalog

Walnut Acres Organic Farms
Penns Creek, PA 17862
(800) 433-3993
natural foods, extensive selection—catalog

The Mail Order Catalog
P.O. Box 180
Summertown, TN 38483
(800) 695-2241, (615) 964-3518—fax
textured vegetable protein, pure gluten powder, nutritional yeast, low-fat soymilk powder

Arrowhead Mills, Inc.
P.O. Box 2059
Hereford, TX 79045
(806) 364-0730
grains, beans, flours, cereals, instant seitan

Allergy Resource
195 Huntington Beach Dr.
Colorado Springs, CO 80921
(719) 488-3630
unusual flours, pastas, etc.

G.B. Ratto & Co.
821 Washington St.
Oakland, CA 94607
(800) 325-3483
grains, beans, flours, international condiments and vinegars, etc.

◆◆◆

Asian, Middle Eastern, Mexican, and Indian Foods/Spices

The Oriental Pantry
423 Great Road
Acton, MA 01720
(800) 823-0368

Kam Man Food Products
200 Canal St.
New York, NY 10013
(212) 571-0330, (212) 766-9085—fax
Thai and Southeast Asian foods

Port of Siam
5400 Highway 17S
Myrtle Beach, SC 29575
(803) 238-2658
Thai and Southeast Asian foods

Orient Blessing Groceries
1513 Church Ave.
Nashville, TN 37203
(615) 327-3682
Indian foods

Canadian Mail Order Sources

Kohinoor International Foods
1438 Gerrard St., E.
Toronto, Ont. M4L I7H
(416) 461-4432
Indian foods, spices, legumes, rice. Will ship COD
anywhere in Canada. Prepaid & credit cards accepted.
Call for prices and ordering information. No catalog.

Que Pasa Mexican Foods
3315 Cambie St.
Vancouver, BC V5K 2W6
(604) 874-0064—orders, (604) 737-7673—fax
Extensive source of chiles, spices, Latin American food
products, tortillas, books, etc. Catalog. Prepaid & credit
cards accepted.

Rafal Spice Company
2521 Russell St.
Detroit, MI 48207
(800) 228-4276

Bangkok Grocery
1021 W. Lawrence
Chicago, IL 60640
(312) 784-0001, (312) 784-2904—fax

India Gifts and Foods
1031 West Belmont Ave.
Chicago, IL 60650
(312) 348-4392

Ta Lin Supermarket
230 Louisiana Blvd., SE
Albuquerque, NM 87108
(505) 268-0206
Thai and Southeast Asian foods

Los Chileros de Nuevo Mexico
P.O. Box 6215
Santa Fe, NM 87502
(505) 471-6967, (505) 473-7306—fax
chiles, Mexican foods—catalog

Choices Market ("Natural Foods for Less")
2627 W. 16th Ave.
Vancouver, BC V6K 3C2
(604) 736-0009, (604) 736-0011—fax
No catalog, but will take phone or fax orders and ship
COD anywhere in Canada. Prepaid & credit cards
accepted. Natural foods, soyfoods, allergy products,
ethnic foods, spices, organic foods, vegan products.
Discounts on volume buying. Friendly service.

Index

◇◇◇

Ask your store to carry these books, or you may order directly from:

The Book Publishing Company
P.O. Box 99
Summertown, TN 38483

Or call: 1-800-695-2241
Please add $2.50 per book
for shipping

by Bryanna Clark Grogan:
20 Minutes To Dinner $12.95
Almost No-Fat Cookbook 12.95
Almost No-Fat Holiday Cookbook 12.95

◇◇◇◇◇◇◇◇◇◇◇◇◇◇◇◇◇

Chef Neil's International Vegetarian Cookbook $5.00
Cookin' Healthy with One Foot Out the Door 8.95
Ecological Cooking: Recipes to Save the Planet 10.95
Fabulous Beans 9.95
Foods Can Save Your Life 9.95
Foods That Cause You To Lose Weight 12.95
From the Global Kitchen 10.95
Good Time Eating In Cajun Country 9.95
Health Promoting Cookbook 12.95
Holiday Diet Cookbook 9.95
Indian Vegetarian Cooking at Your House 12.95
Instead of Chicken, Instead of Turkey 9.95
Judy Brown's Guide to Natural Foods Cooking 10.95
New Farm Vegetarian Cookbook 8.95
Now & Zen Epicure 17.95
Nutritional Yeast Cookbook 9.95
Olive Oil Cookery 10.95
Peaceful Palate 15.00
Physician's Slimming Guide 5.95
Shoshoni Cookbook 12.95
The Sprout Garden 8.95
Solar Cooking 8.95
Soyfoods Cookery 9.95
Table for Two 12.95
Tofu Cookery 15.95
TVP® Cookbook 7.95
Uncheese Cookbook 11.95
Vegan Vittles 11.95
Vegetarian Cooking for People with Diabetes 10.95